High Shelf

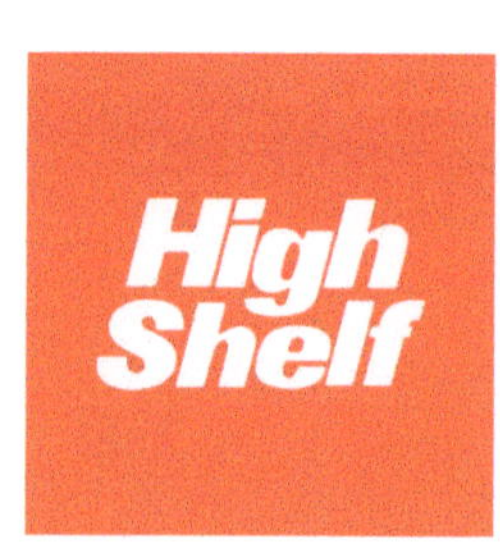

High Shelf* XXXIV. *September 2021.
Portland, Oregon.
Copyright 2021, High Shelf Press

ISBN: 978-1-952869-40-2

Cover Image by Chris Boyko
Design and Layout by C. M. Tollefson
Editing by David Seung & C. M. Tollefson

With special thanks to:
Eric Hoskins & Megan Kim.

High Shelf XXXXIV

September 2021

"... my body landlocked, a house of healing.
how what taunted taught me the most.
and it goes, and it goes, and it goes... "
Vanessa Grixti

"... I check the clock—
as always, there's time..."

Will Dolben

Table Of Contents

A girl can dream,   9
    Courtney Messenbaugh
River Ice   1
    Steve Geer
I am not a respite   2
    Vanessa Grixti
there's a stranger in my body and she won't let me go   2
    Natalia A. Pagán Serrano
I Wish I Had Said It   2
    Kathryn Matheson
NOTHING IS PERFECT   3
    Will Dolben
Train Graveyard (Uyuni, Bolivia)   3
    Jeremiah Gilbert
When We Left Fort Recovery   4
    Robert McDonald
Plenty Some One   4
    Chris Andrews
Aghast, Innocence, and Intensity   4
    Paul Reynolds
Split   5
    Melinda Freudenberger
Ahistorical   5
    Kirsten Hemmy
Dreaming   5
    Diamante Lavendar
ACT Practice Test in the Time of COVID   6
    Candice Kelsey
Exercise I: Definitions   6
    Alex Mepham
Surrealism   6
    Chris Boyko
Hospitoritory +   7
    Garry Egger

To: Enchanted Spirit 1111 Channeled Intuitive Clairaudient Tarot Reader   81
on YouTube Fr: A recently awakened from the dark night of the soul
superfan
     Amy Randall
Two Fables about Recovery   83
     Alex Shapiro
Ekphrastic Challenge   84
     artist & author

A girl can dream,

Courtney Messenbaugh

I think to myself, after he tells me
the story of Orpheus &
Eurydice. He hears love &
dedication, I hear captivity. I
am quiet. The snow is quiet as
it falls from the inky sky. We
walk at night now, the day is
garish & exposes too much.
In the dark, the dry snow
beneath our feet, is like sugar
that shushes us with every step,
reminding us of sweetness. That
it still exists in this world. My
cheeks flush, my heart pounds,
my pulse quickens, as if we're
making love, but we are not
making love. We are walking
in the frigid night because
the day is too bright &
our dreams are too far.

River Ice

Steve Geer

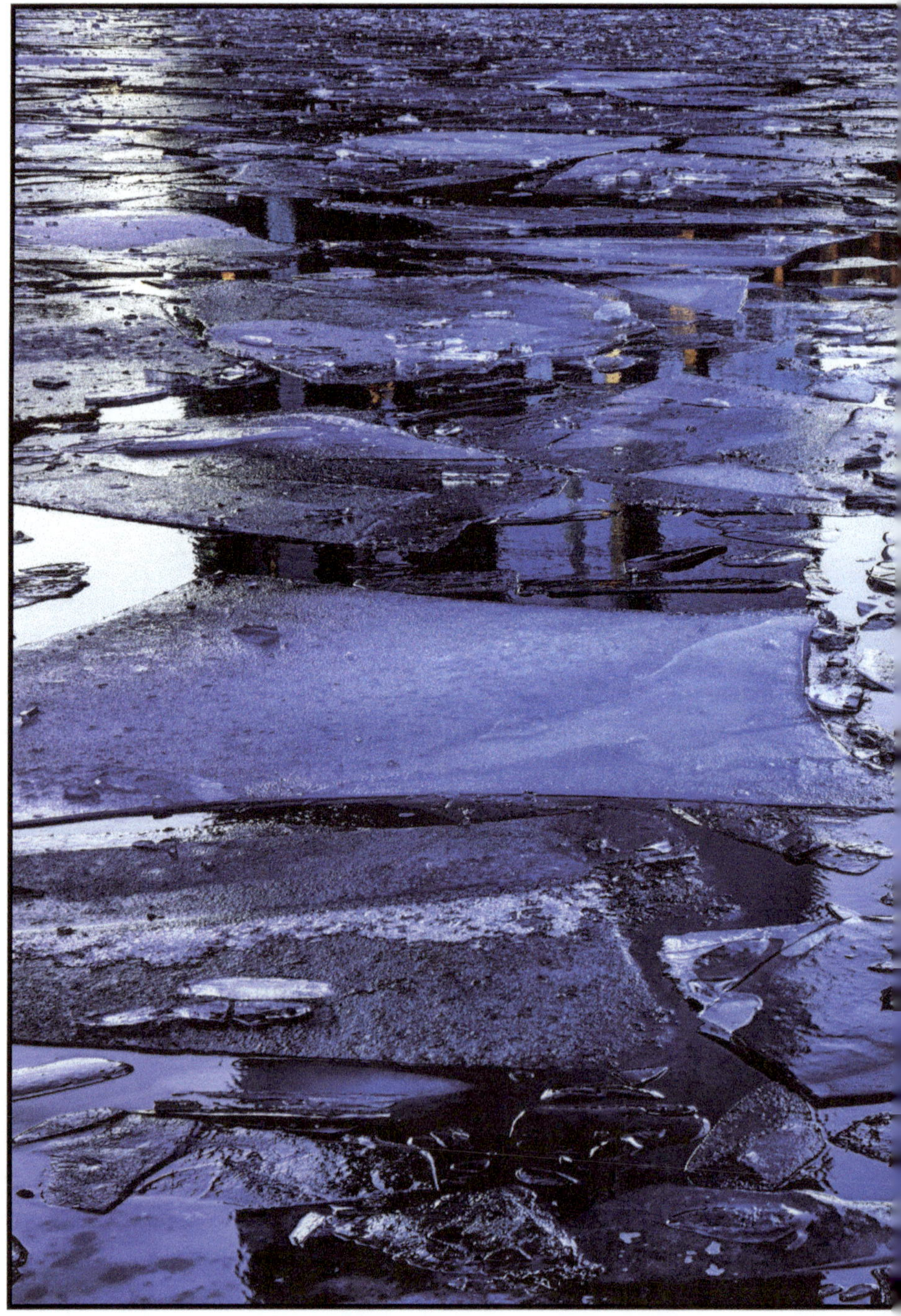

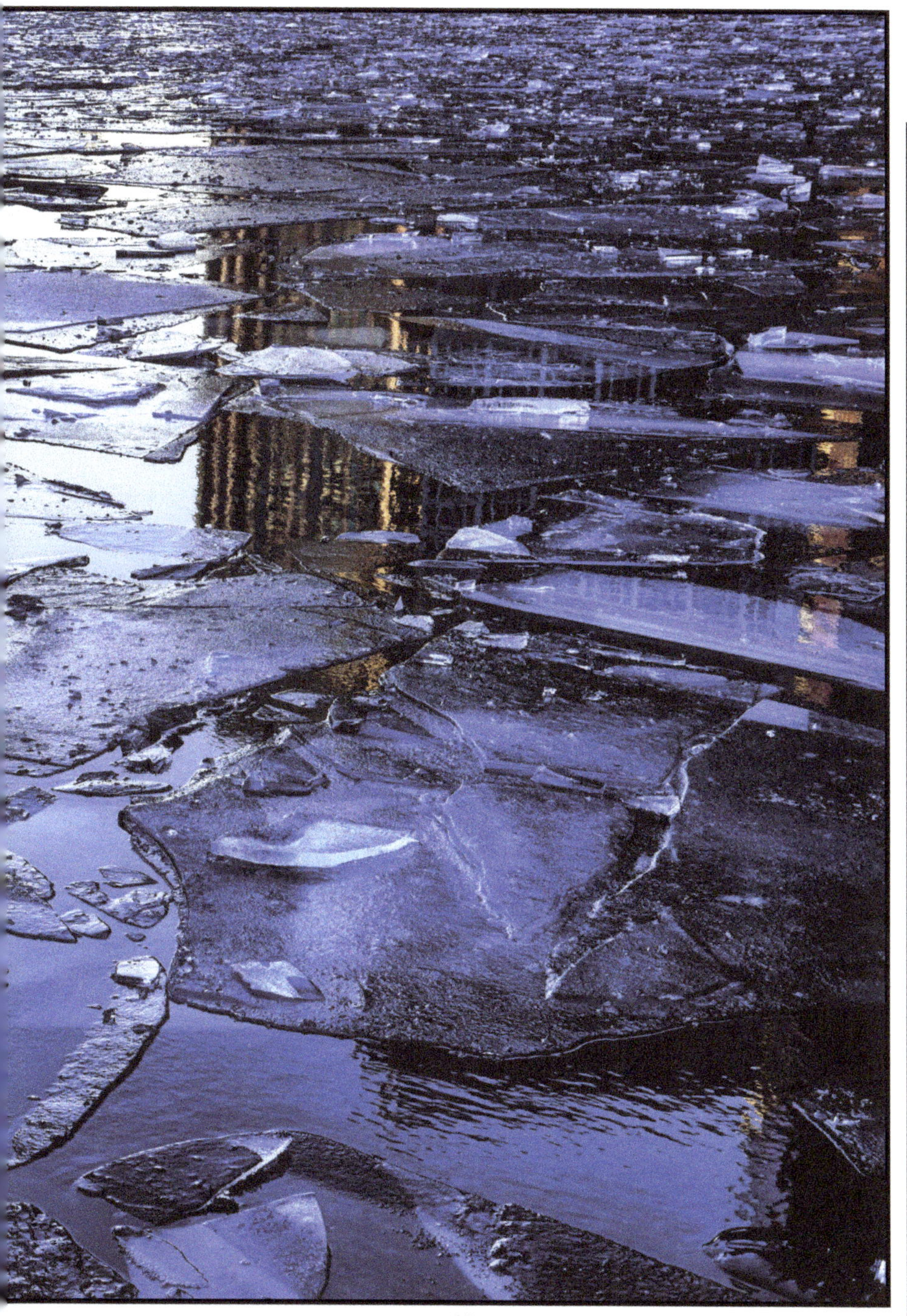

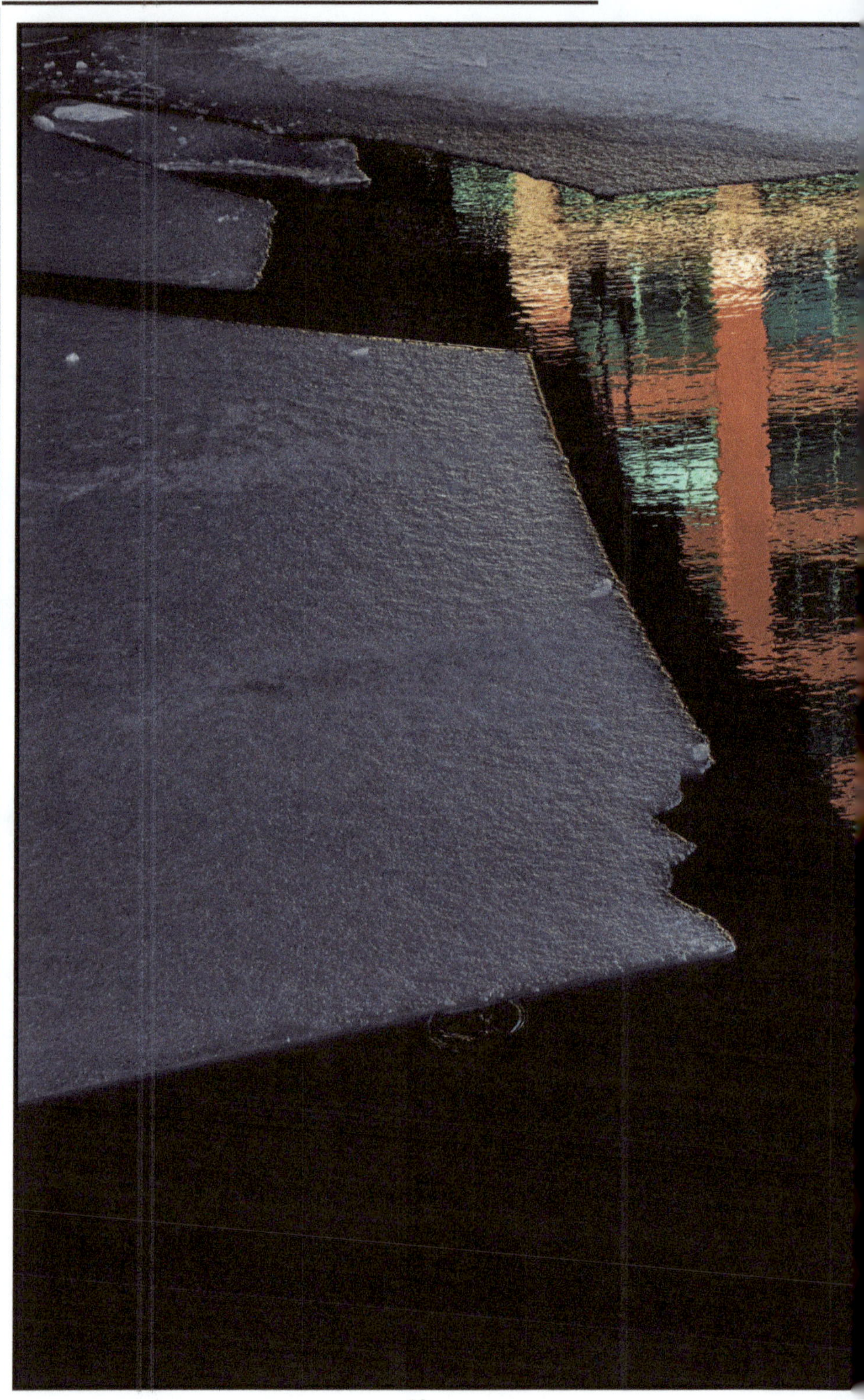

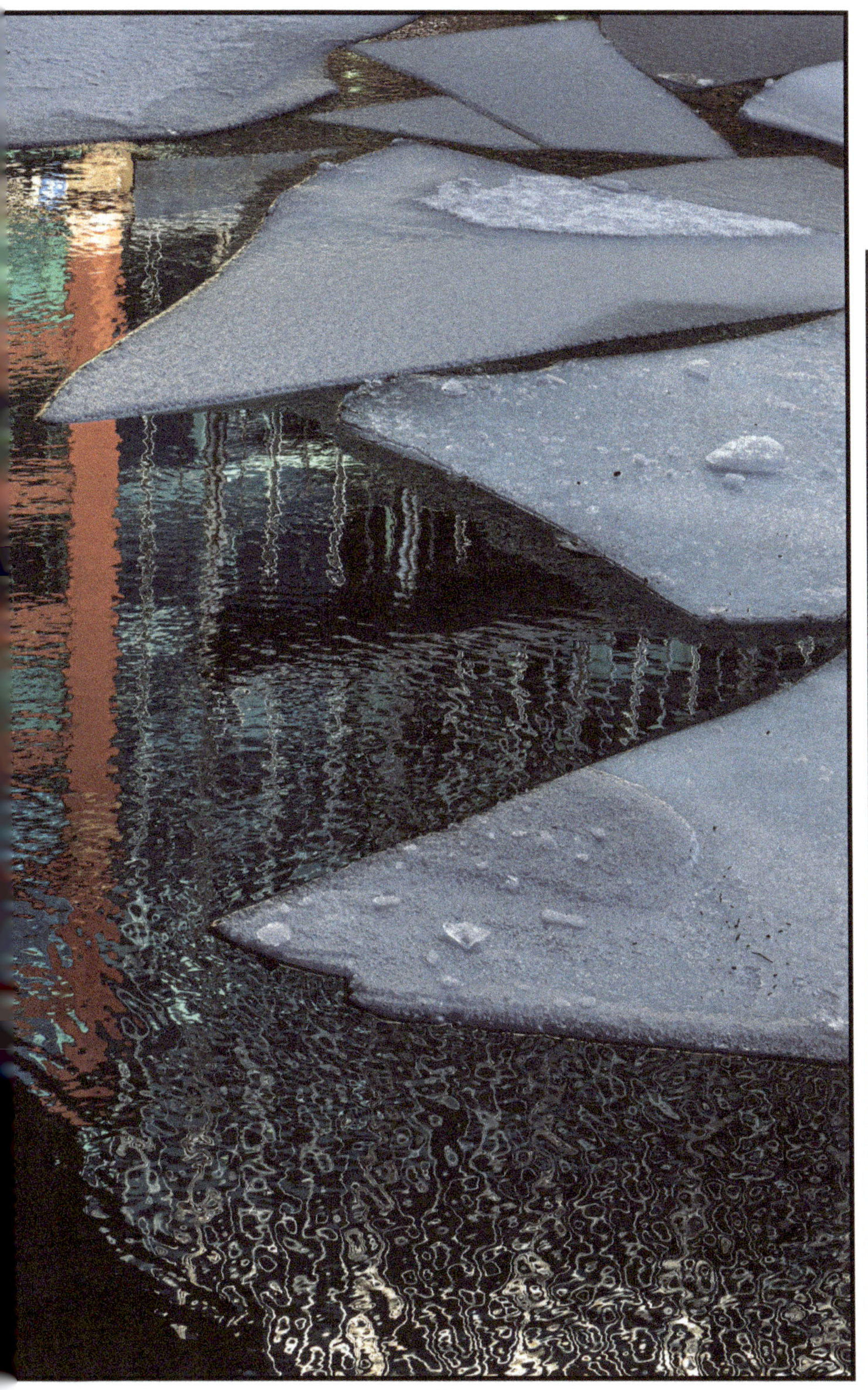

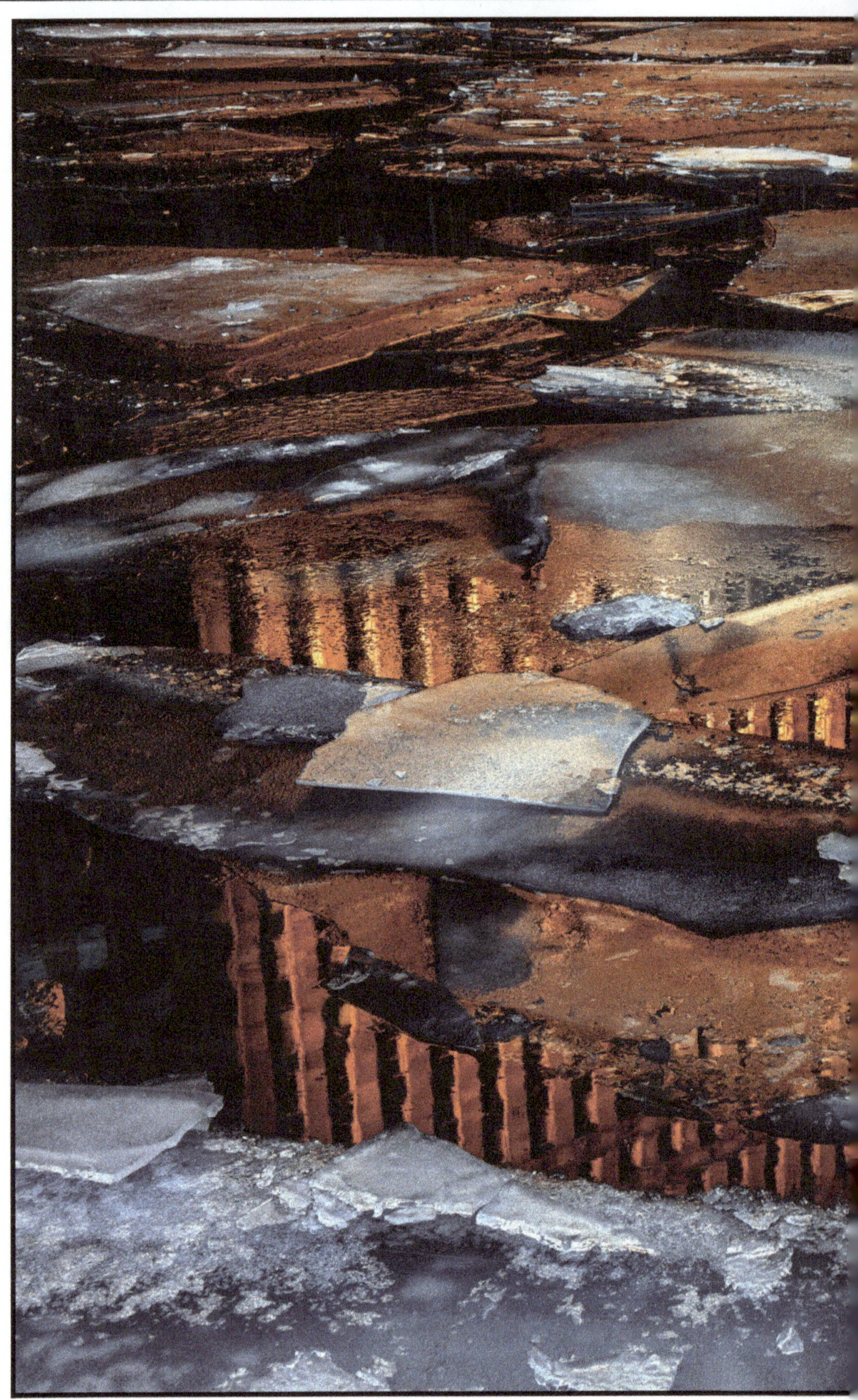

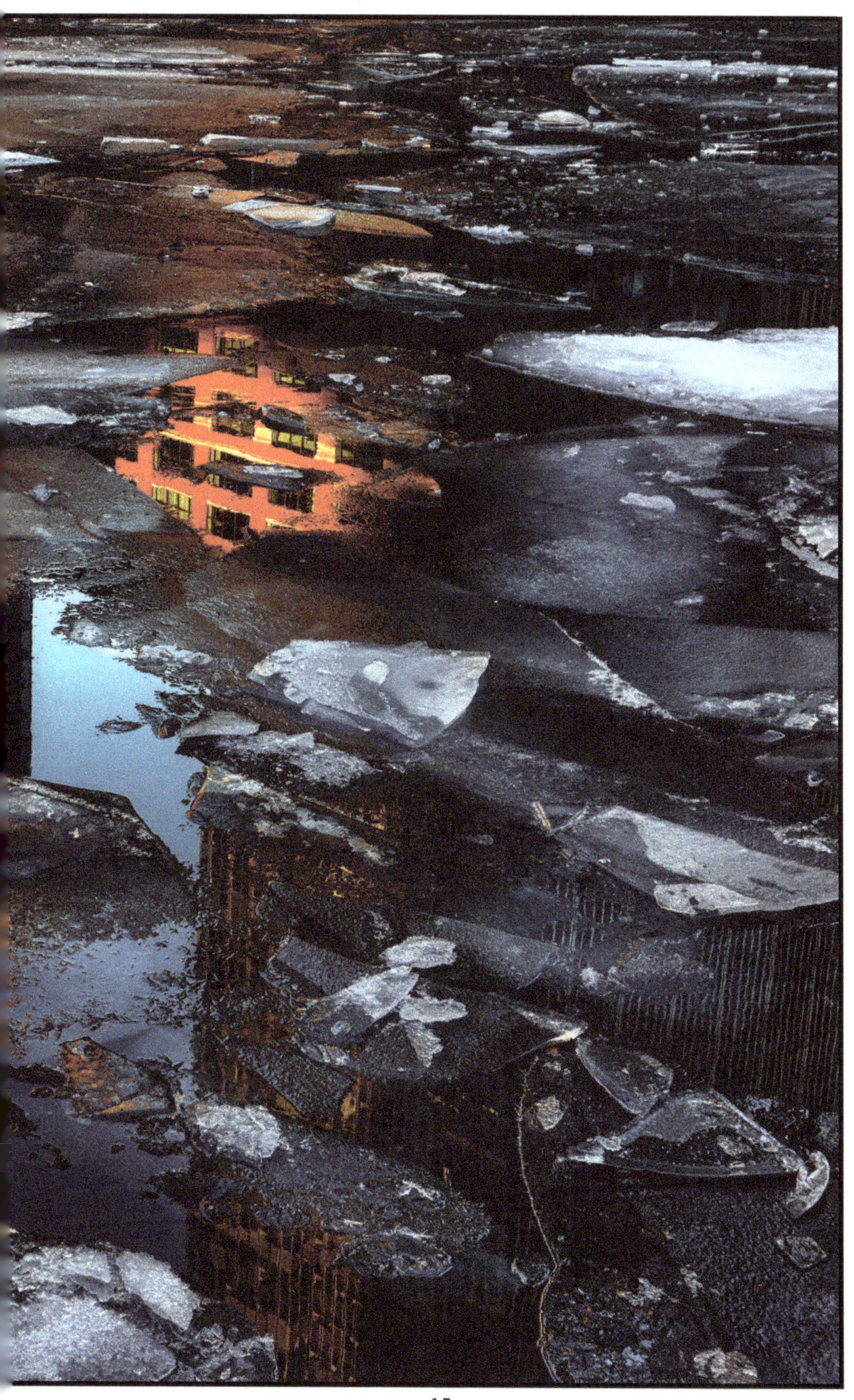

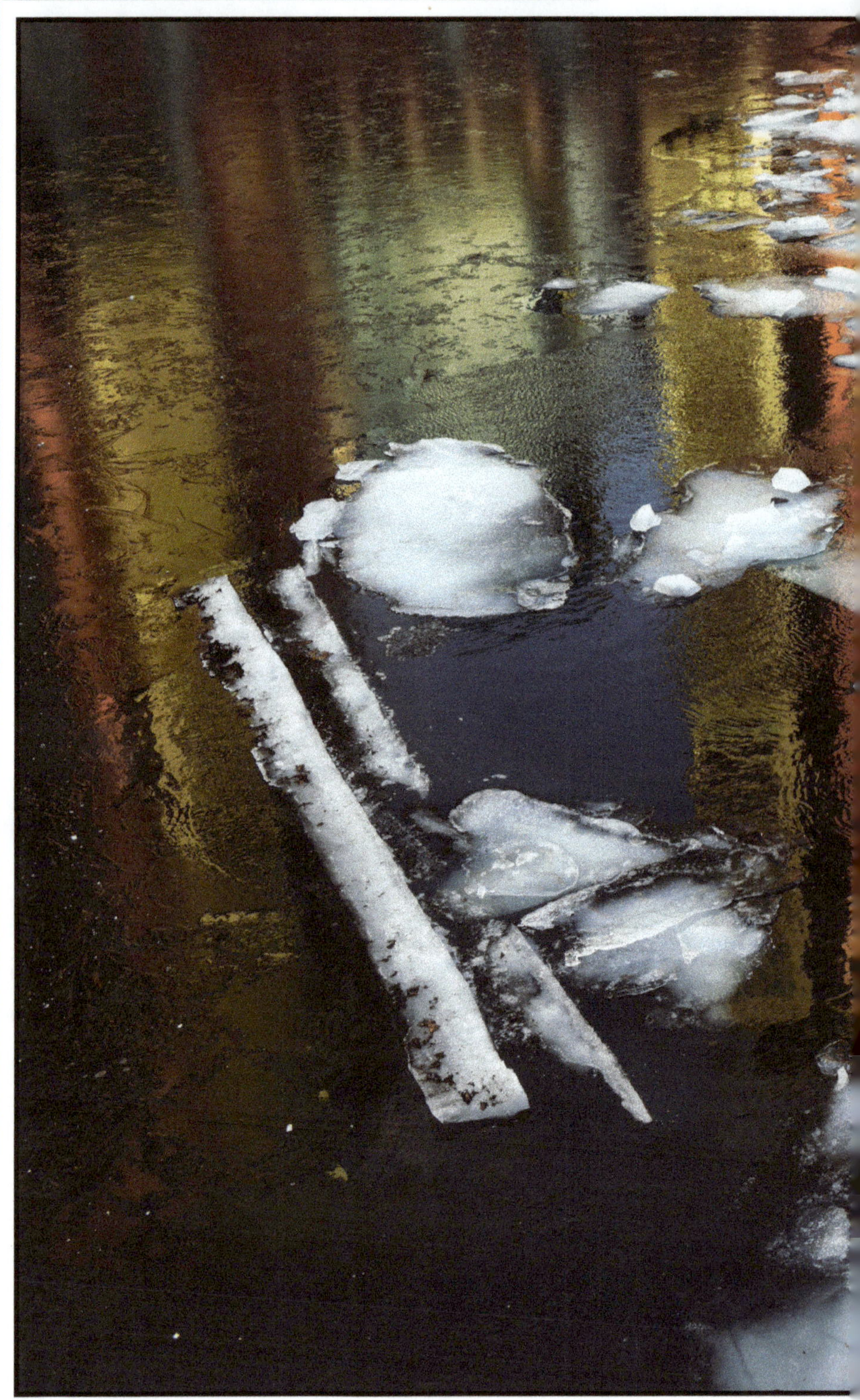

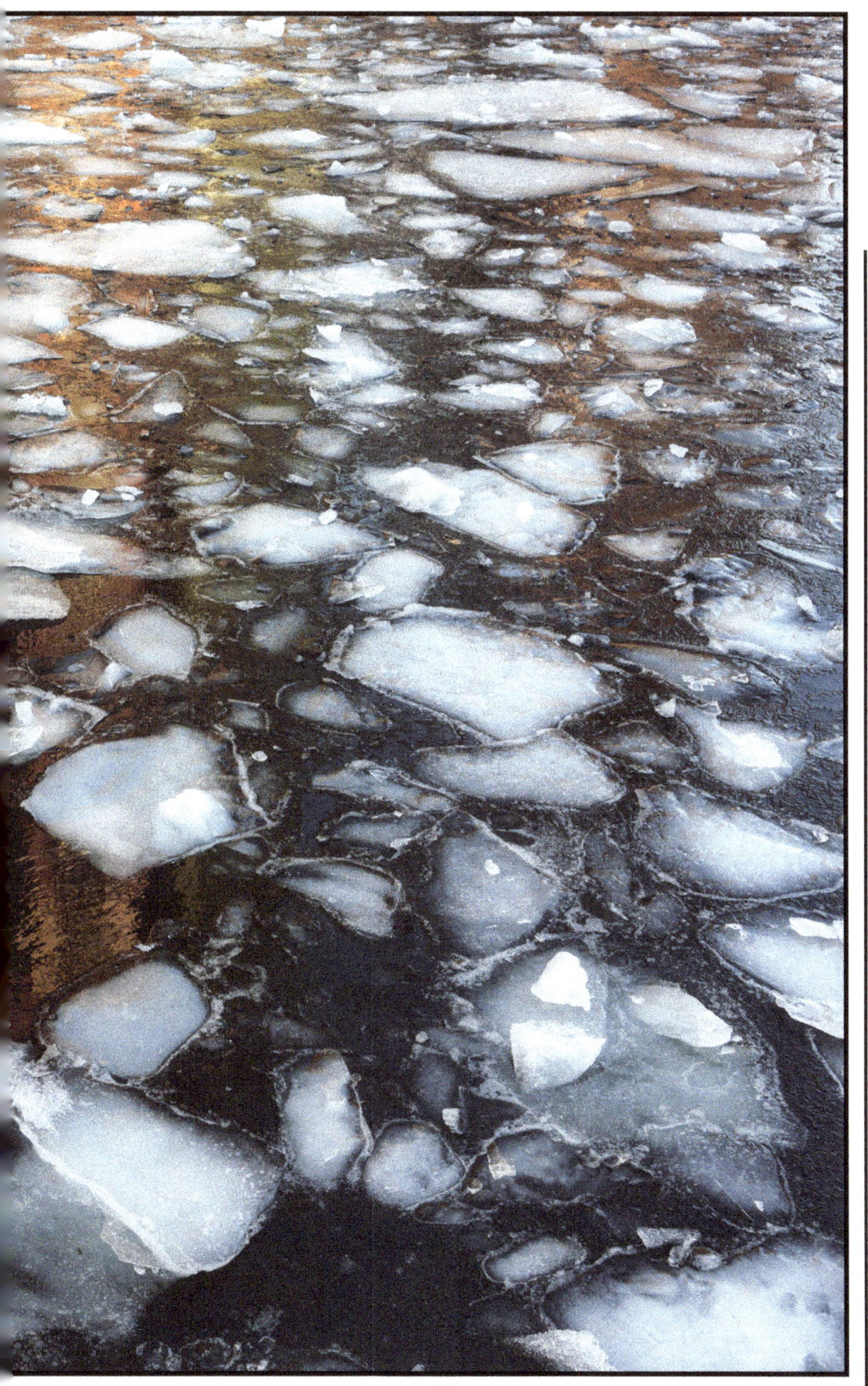

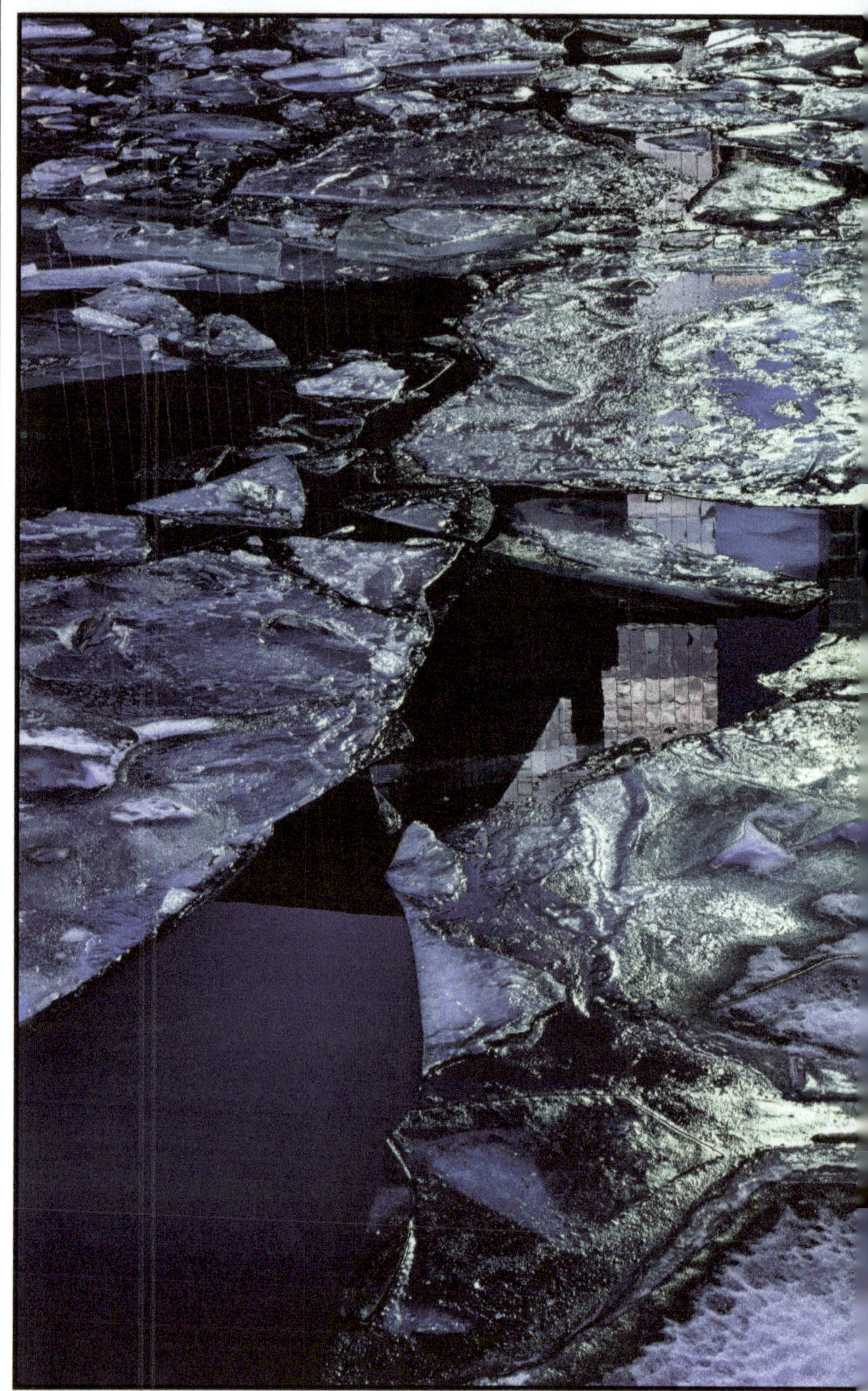

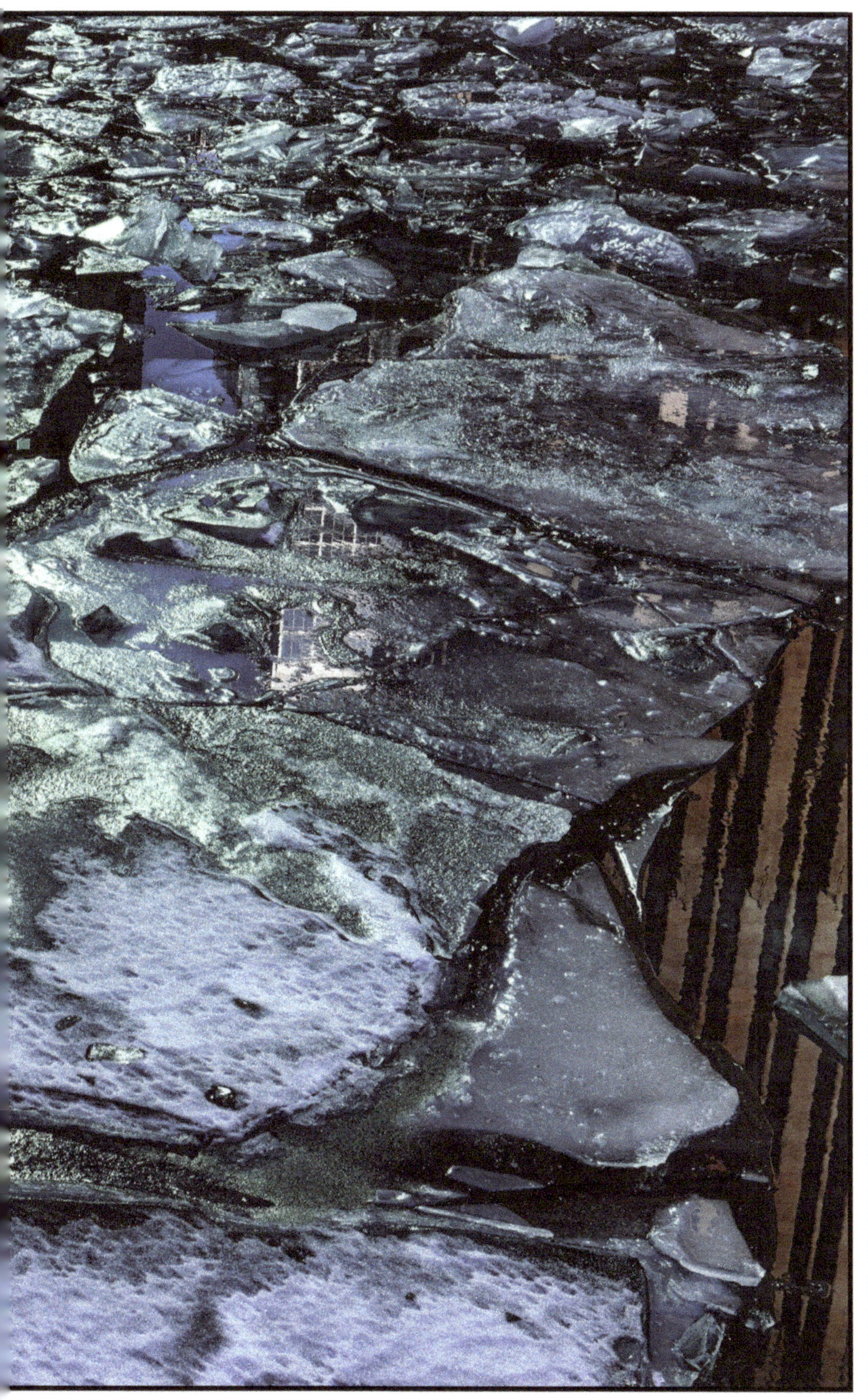

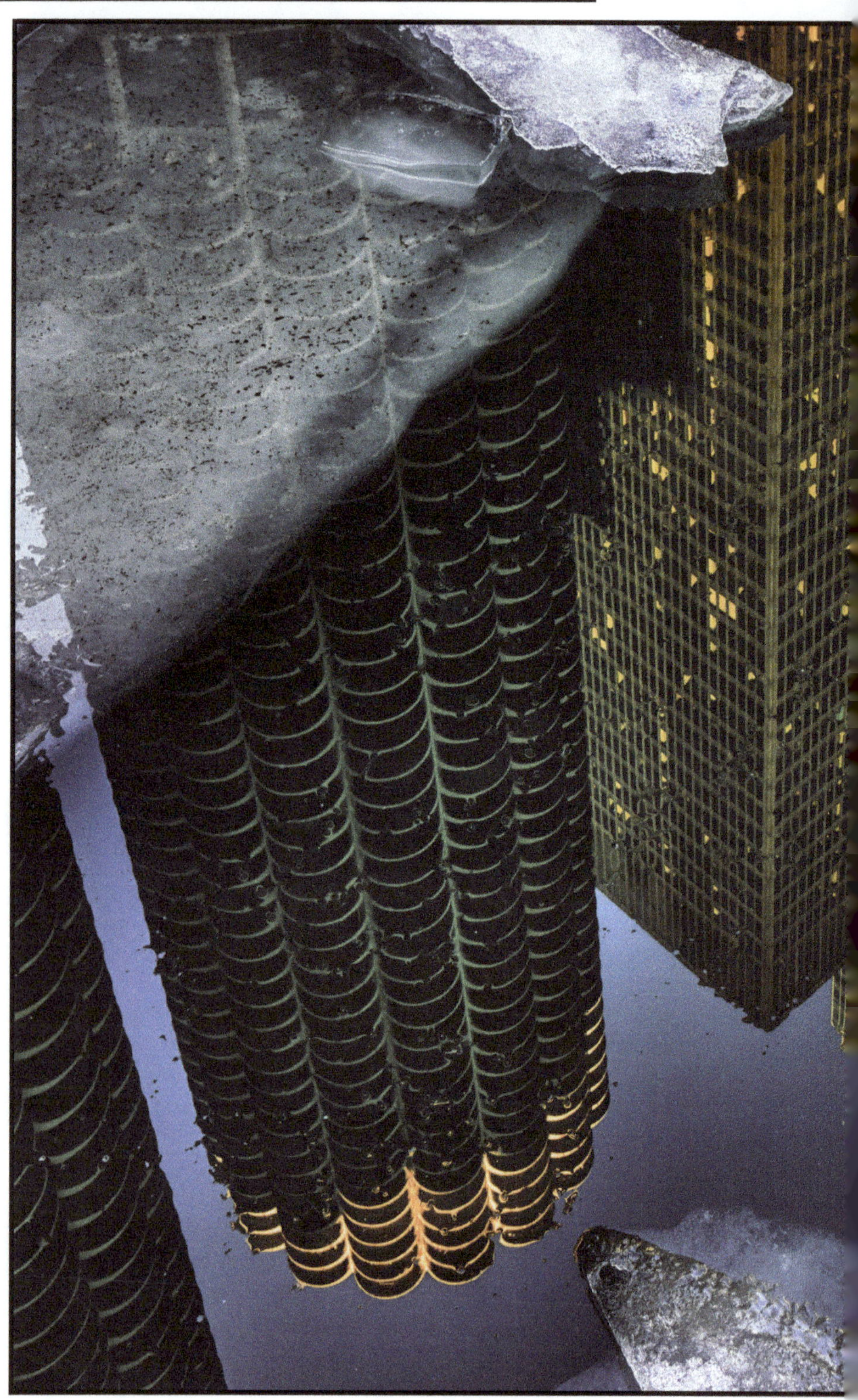

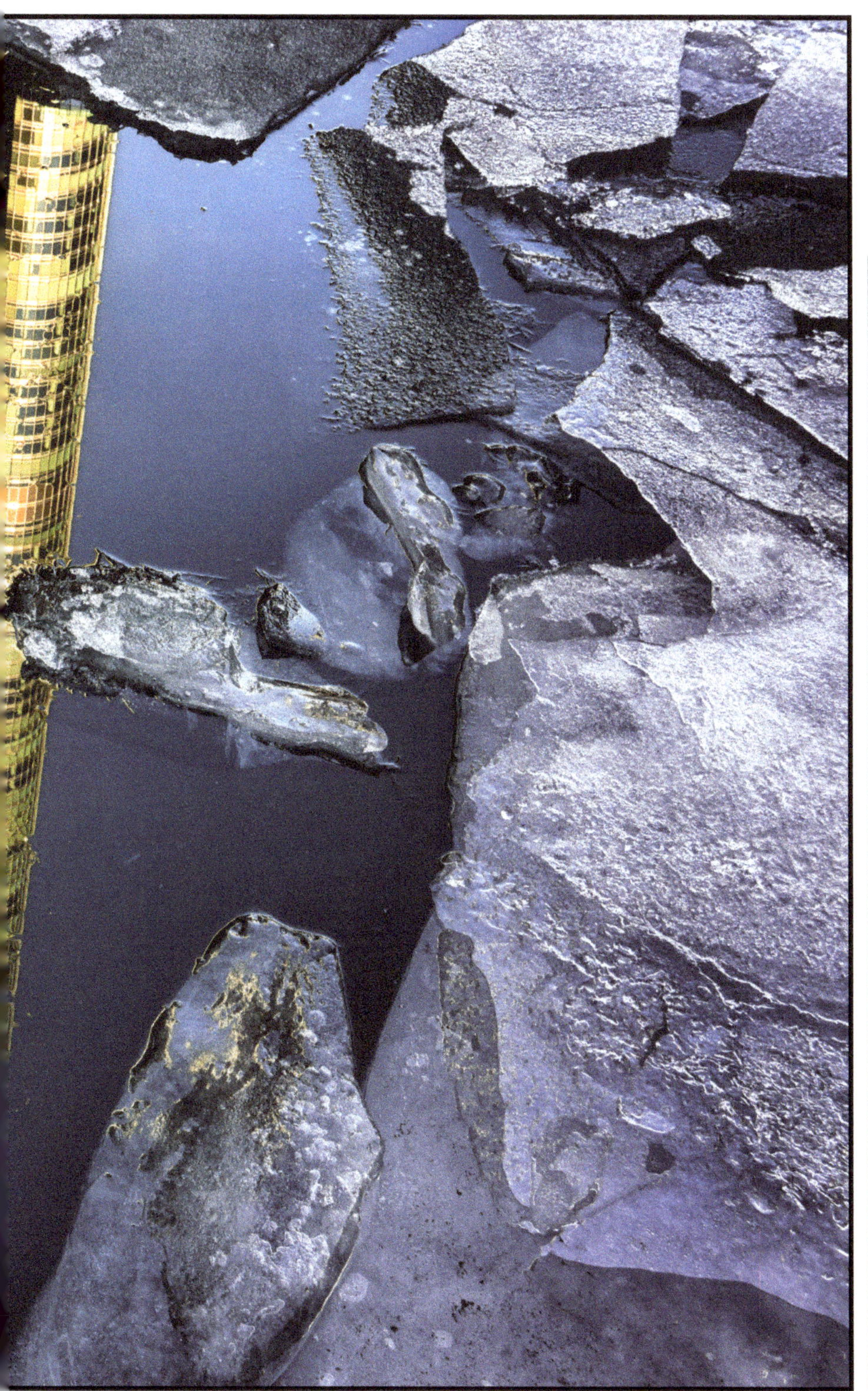

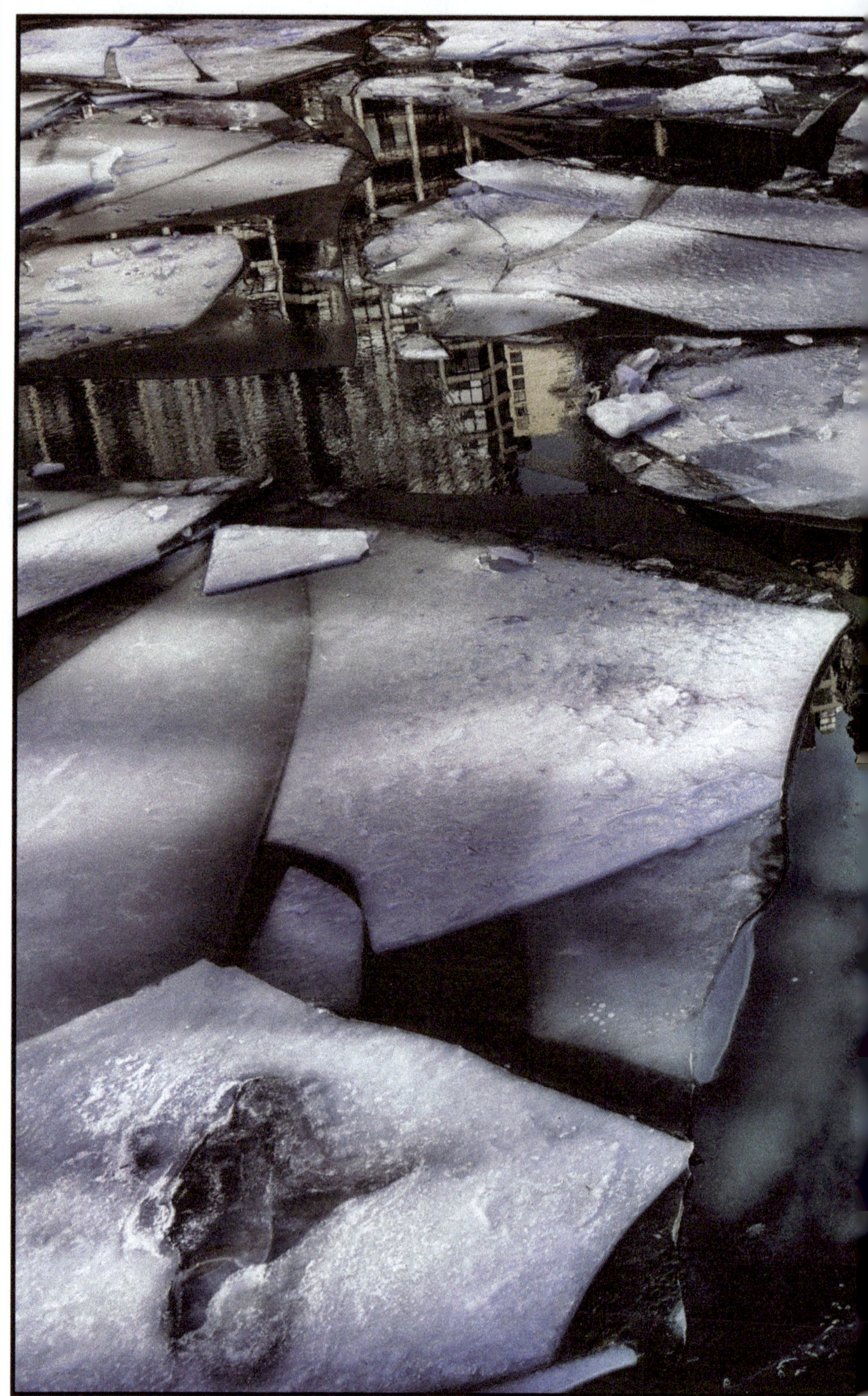

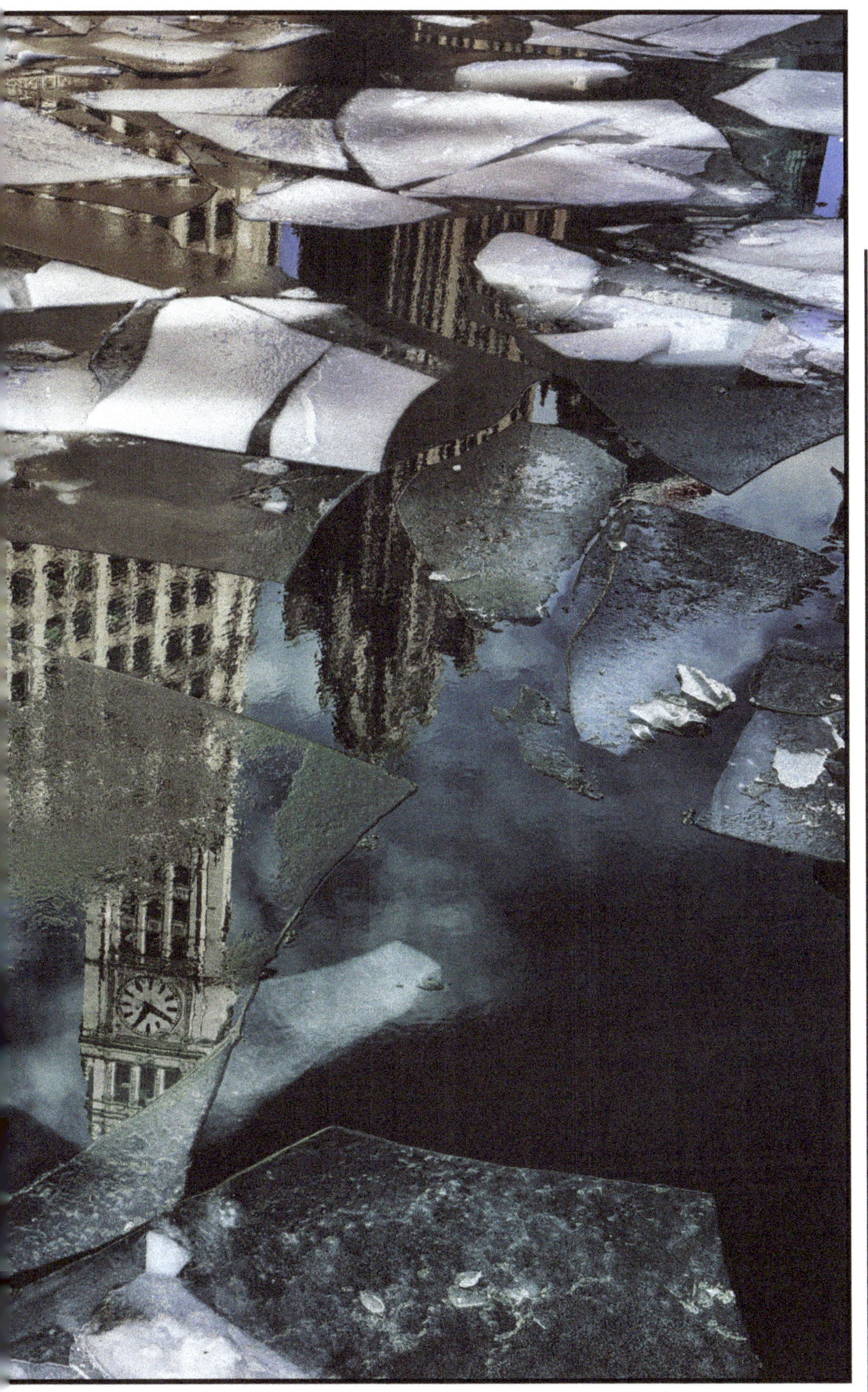

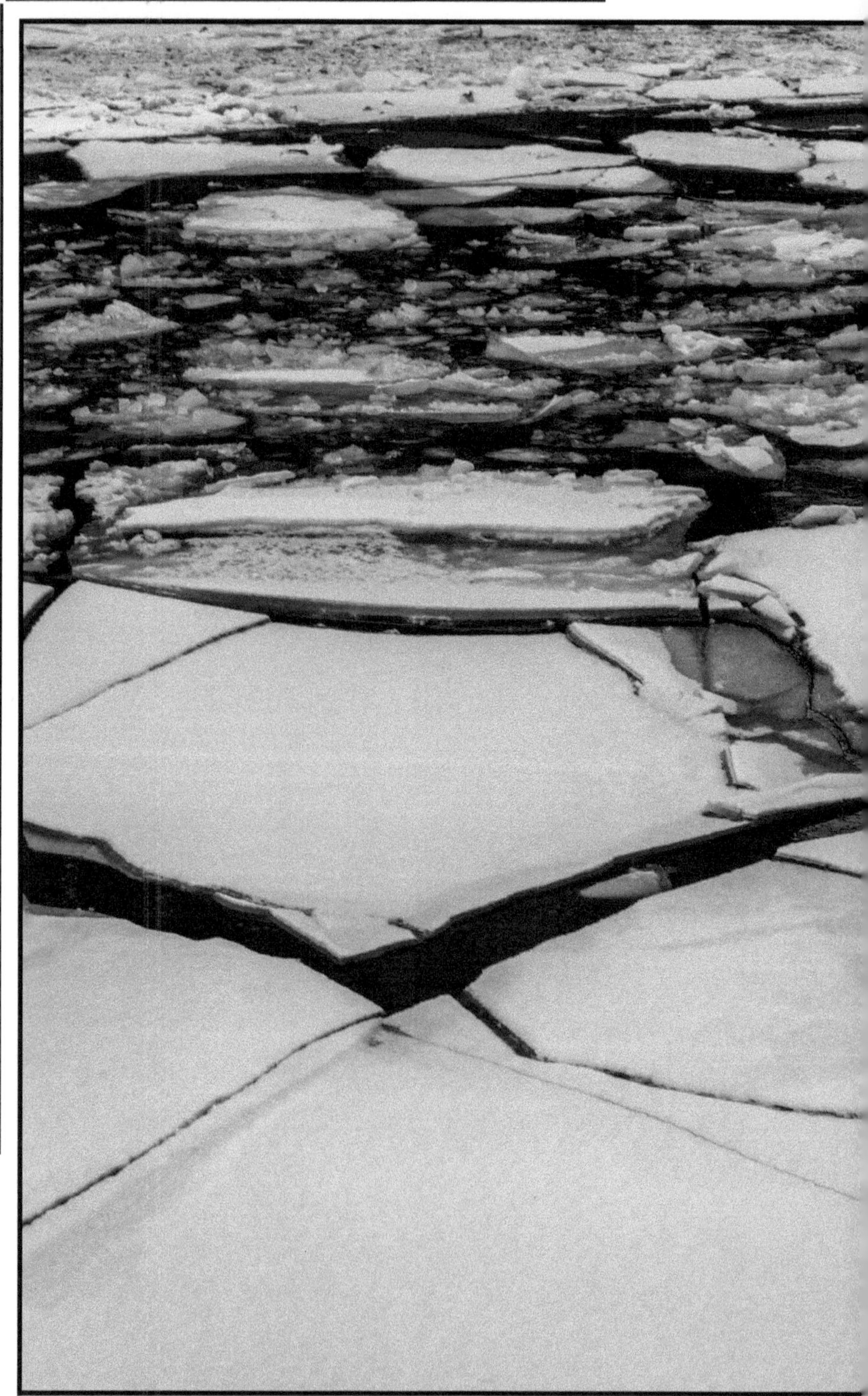

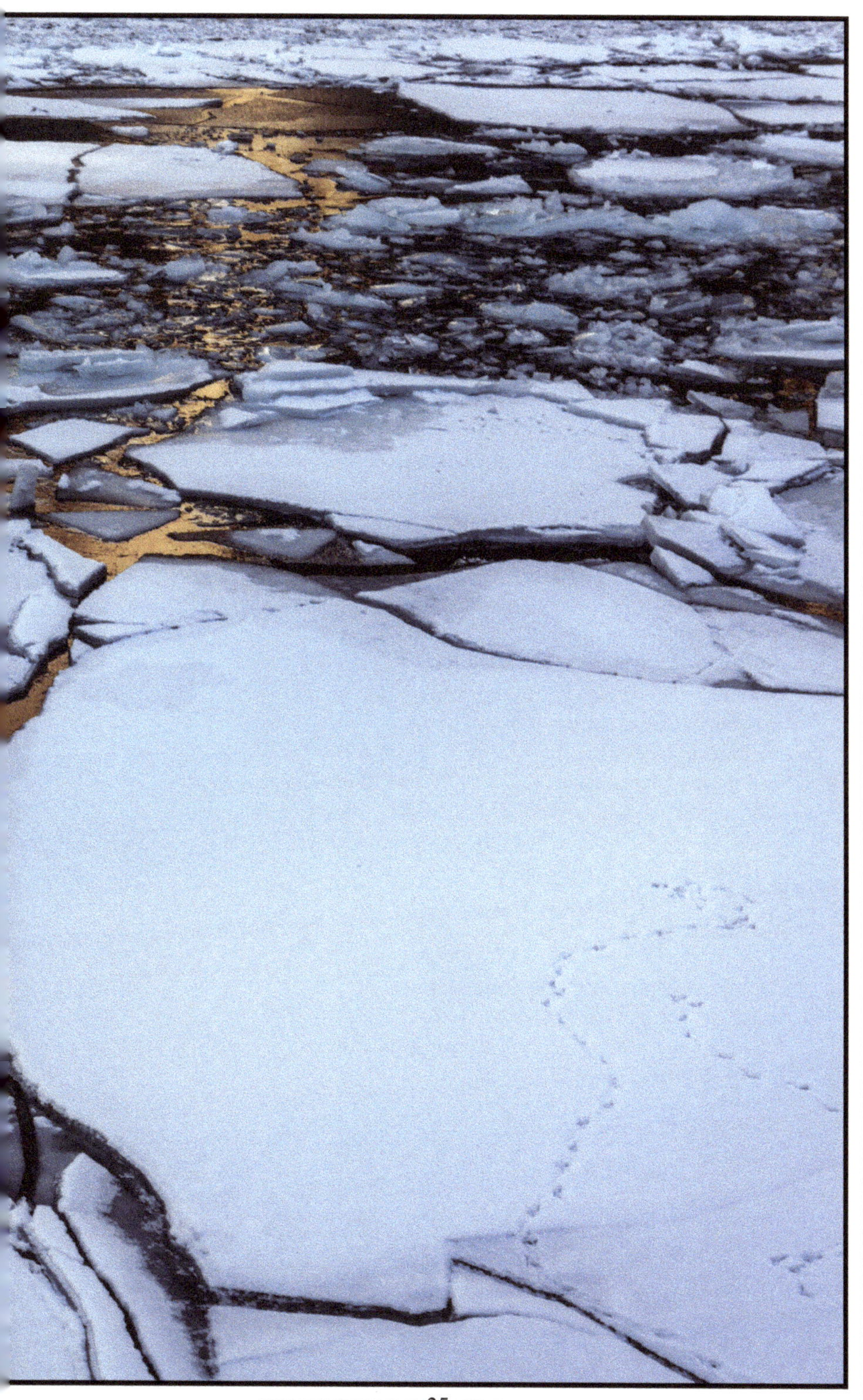

I am not a respite

Vanessa Grixti

for the pain of men, yet here I am,
my years blended into remedies,
my body landlocked, a house of healing.
how what taunted taught me the most.
and it goes, and it goes, and it goes:
there is no mending the cold steel of cruelty,
only understanding, so I swallow the ceiling,
the threshold becomes me.
now, I can't tell a dance from an argument.
his every accusation acrobatic,
a threat like a tightrope,
the belly of tomorrow growling below.
and I find him there in his weeping,
each sob an orchestration,
a captive inner-child performing.
so I gather him like a mother would, into my chest,
a landscape expansive and warm as forgiveness.
my instincts swaddling my evolution into slumber,
skin raw and salted toiling the tenses of his sorrow.
wisdom spent wrestling egos out of men,
yielding to and of them.
I curl into callous like a cradle, surrender in exhales,
this nocturnal ritual of rebirth.
from above our bed the moon beckons like a tunnel's end,
I must ride this dark towards it.

an exit eclipsed.

I awake wailing into the sun, languageless.
this time, swallowing the sky,
I become the universe, a womb against its wish,
ever-widening, infinite

there's a stranger in my body and she won't let me go

Natalia A. Pagán Serrano

she has twenty pounds on me
and doesn't like you touching her

she does not recognize my love for you
flinches at the feel of your fingers

retreats into my body further
an animal fearing its cage

she frustrates easily, though
she is the one who keeps

shoes under the dining table,
gathers dried-blood wine glasses

behind the TV, she demands
load the dishwasher

empty the litter box
eggs from the market

she'll grimace if you ask
when it is you who says *yes*

yes
yes

yes your knees bent at her feet
she recoils when you touch the overspun

skin under her belly button
yearning for my warmth, and loving

the overspun skin, craving our body
though it is bent at the neck

and flesh accumulates under
the shoulder blades, and somewhere

I've tried to keep myself here
in our body, even when it makes her shiver

even when she refuses to seek the sun
it's me who asks you to use your fingers

yes

to keep the red on this head
to keep me in our body longer

even though it scares you
to see your hands bloody

and I will urge you yes
it is me staring back in the mirror

while we practice this thing
called love

I Wish I Had Said It

Kathryn Matheson

My great-grandmother hated
the color yellow — wouldn't wear it,
no matter the shade,
and when she was dying
she looked like a baby bird,
a fledging, perched to fly.

So, there is that.
Leaning over her bed,
I forgot to say
I was grateful for the lesson.
Yellow clashes
with our hair.

Or the time she called
to say she had been
a wallflower too, and I should
just get out there
and dance.

Drinking scotch
and soda at night
can get you 101 years
so, have a little fun
along the way
and with your hair done
you can have
as many men as you want,
get re-married at 80, fall
in love 17 times,

take up a new hobby
and paint the sky, window boxes,
parrots preening.
Put out a dish of pecans, salty-savory
on top of the picture albums and
curling edges.

And in the breakfast room hangs
a clock that sings a different bird-
song every hour.

10am on the day of her funeral,
the Yellow Warbler chips at the room
and then goes quiet.

NOTHING IS PERFECT

Will Dolben

I wake,
eat applesauce,
prepare to write a perfect poem.
I know this isn't possible,
believe today's the day.

I check the clock—
as always, there's time.

I play the right music,
examine my journals.
I look out the window,
see as much as I can.

I ask myself what the fuck I'm doing.
Shouldn't I be selling houses?
Why does anyone write a poem?

I walk out on the dock.
A gull takes a fish,
flies across the lake,
drowns him in the air.

Train Graveyard (Uyuni, Bolivia)

Jeremiah Gilbert

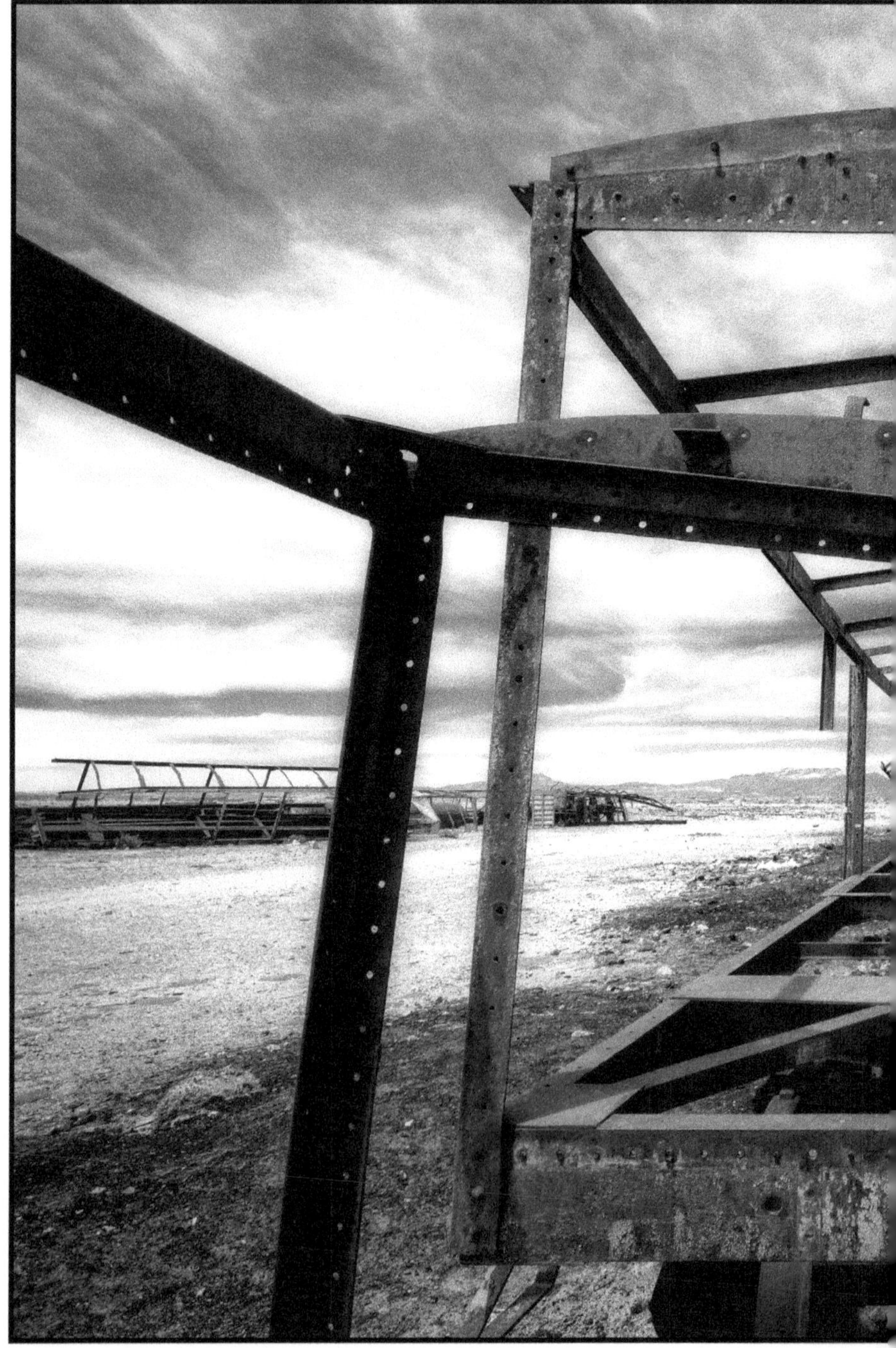

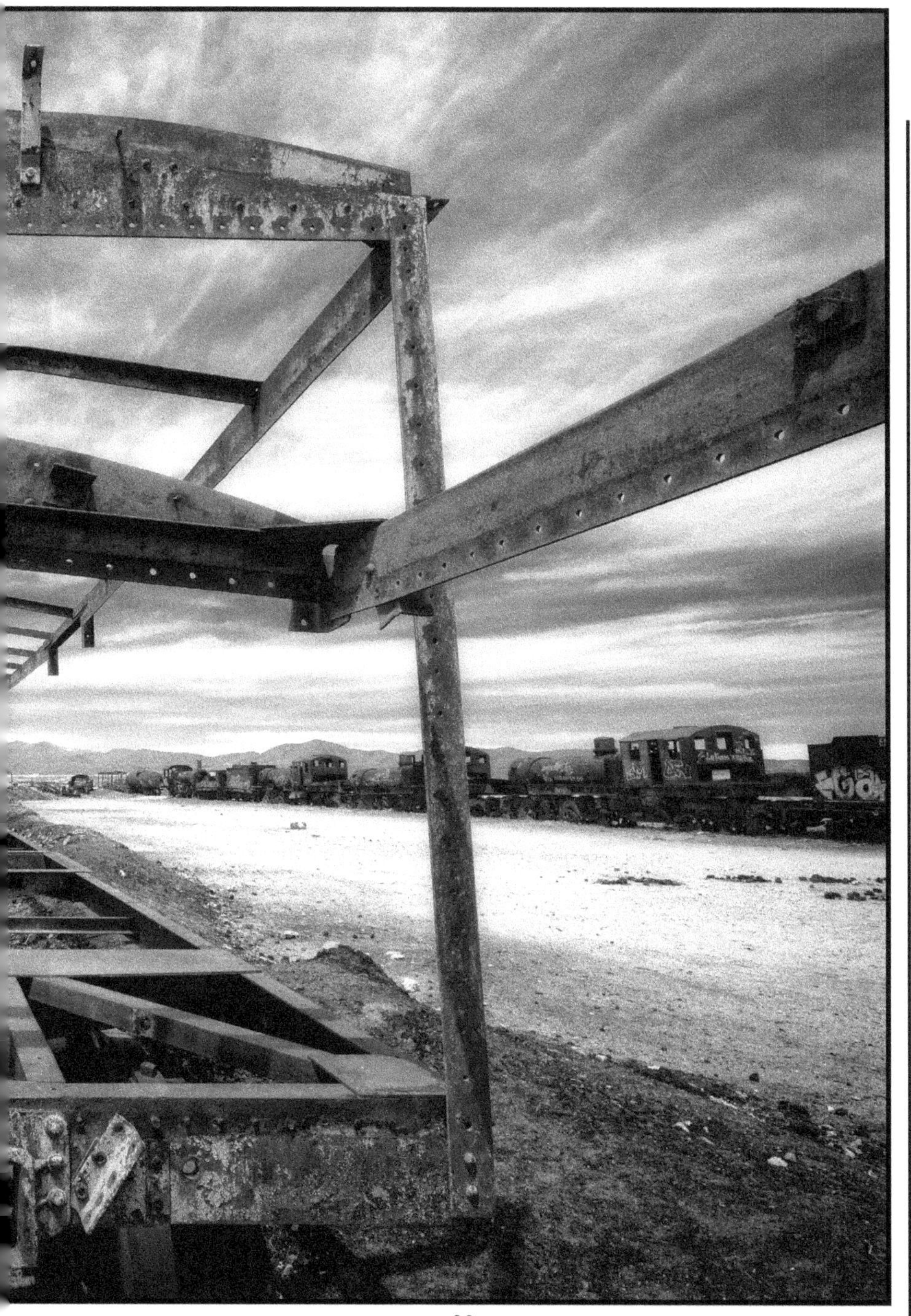

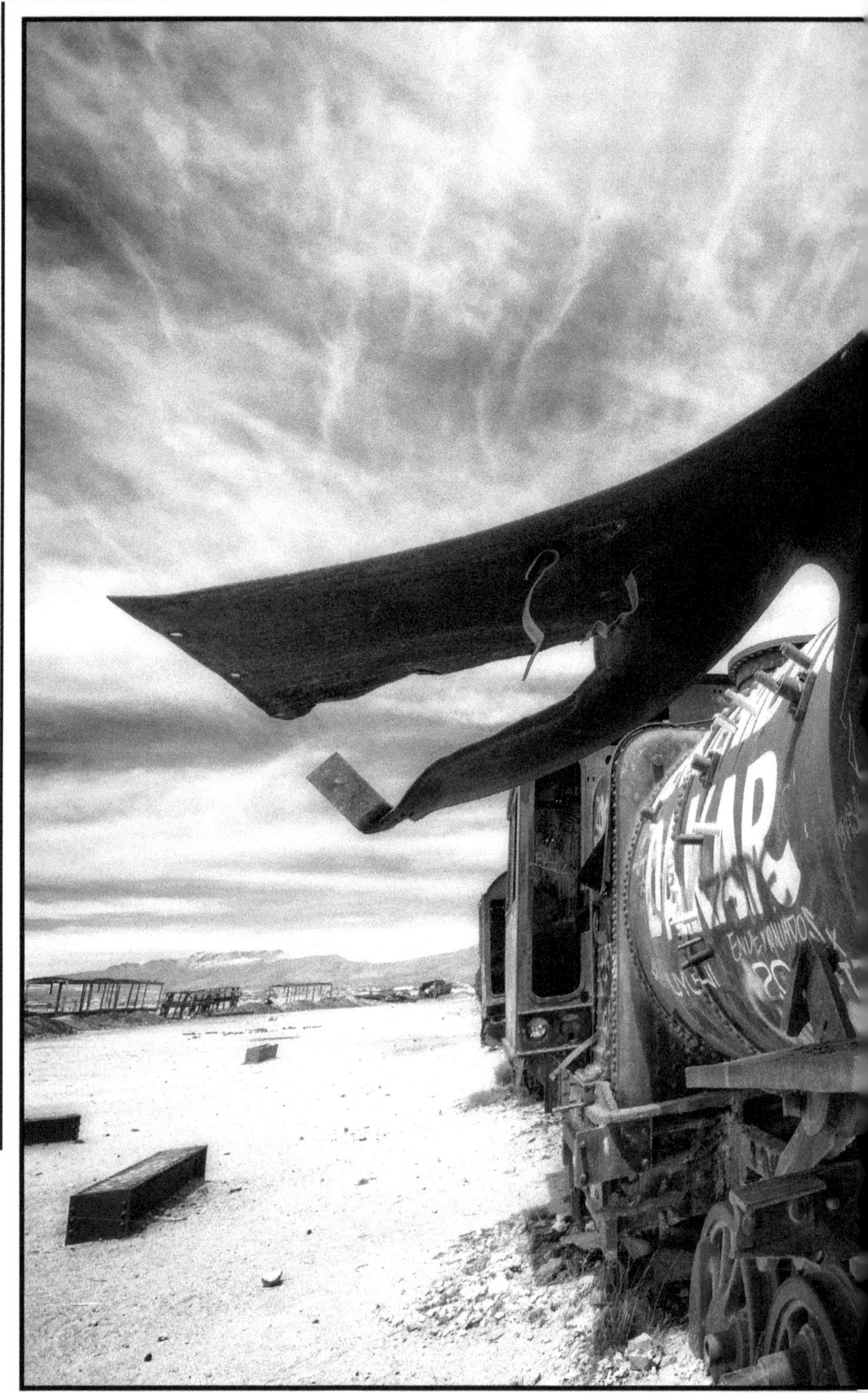

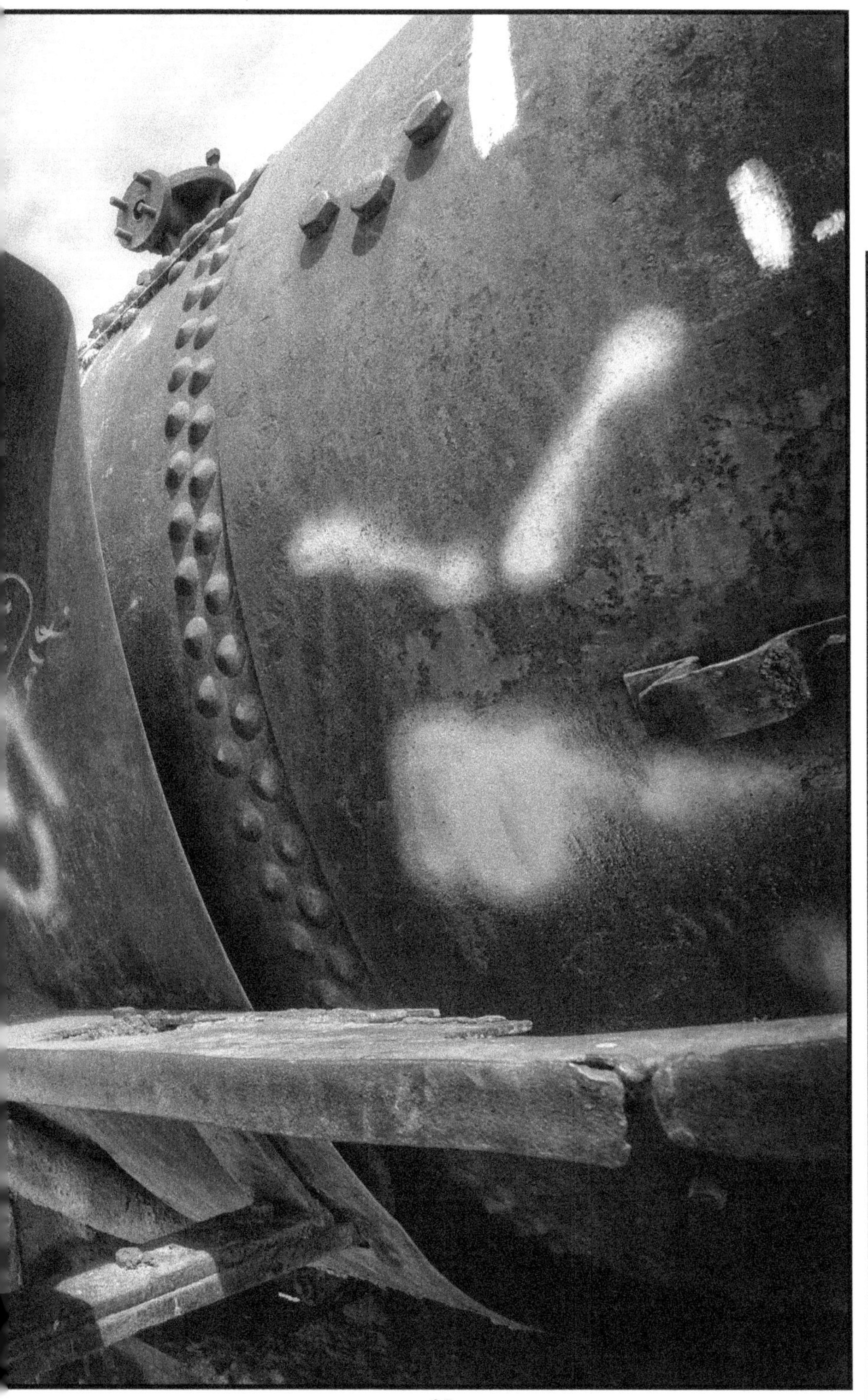

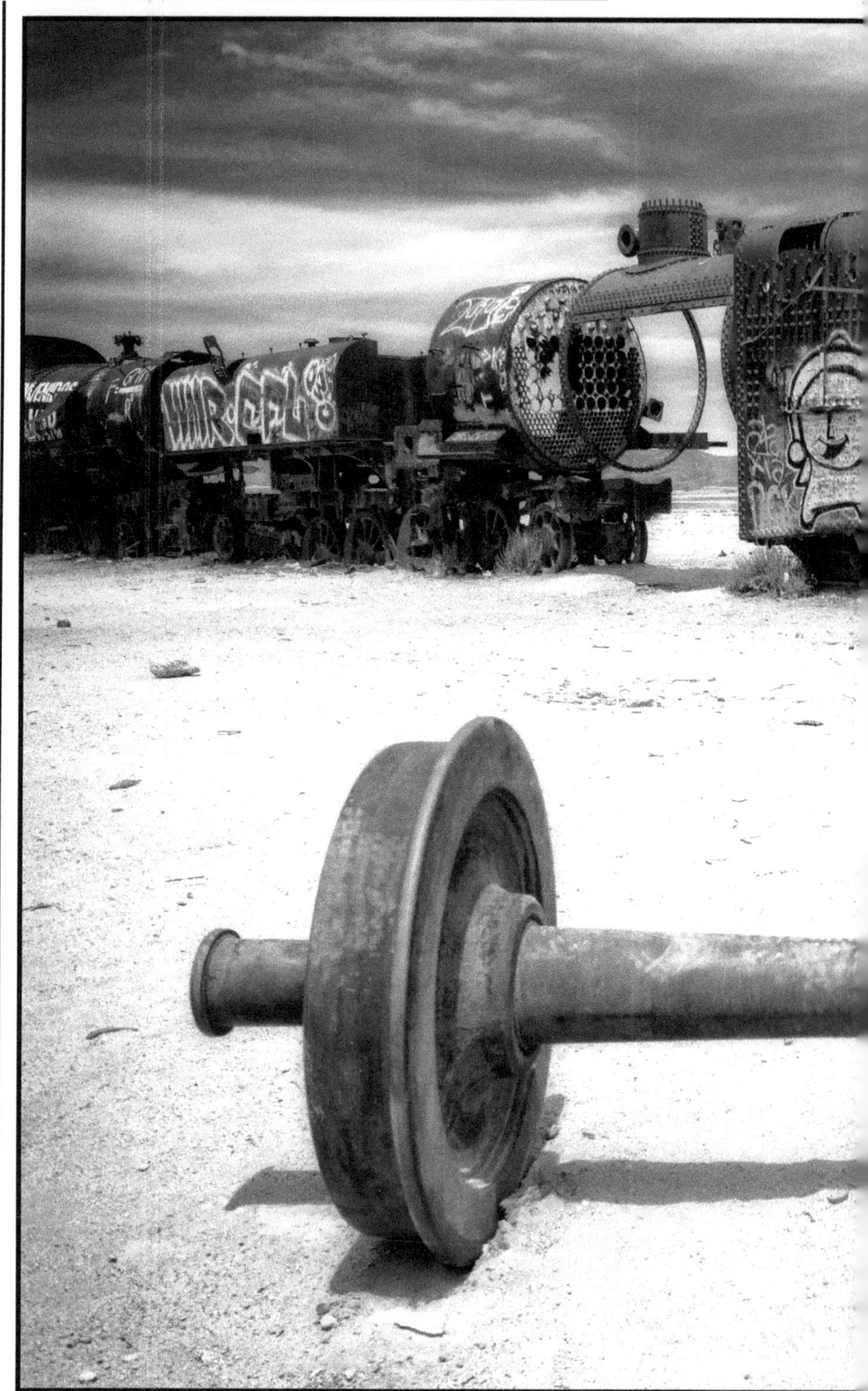

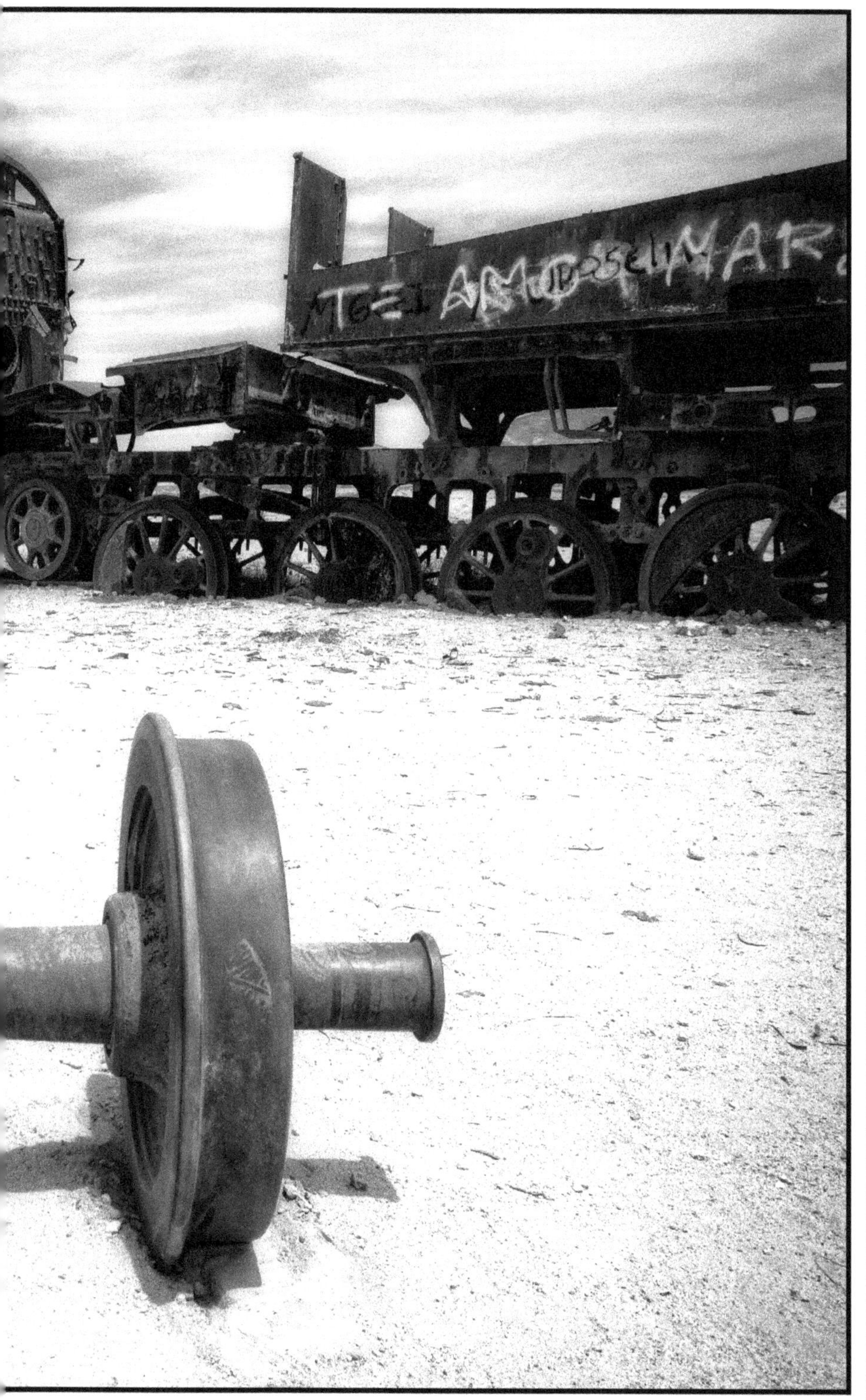

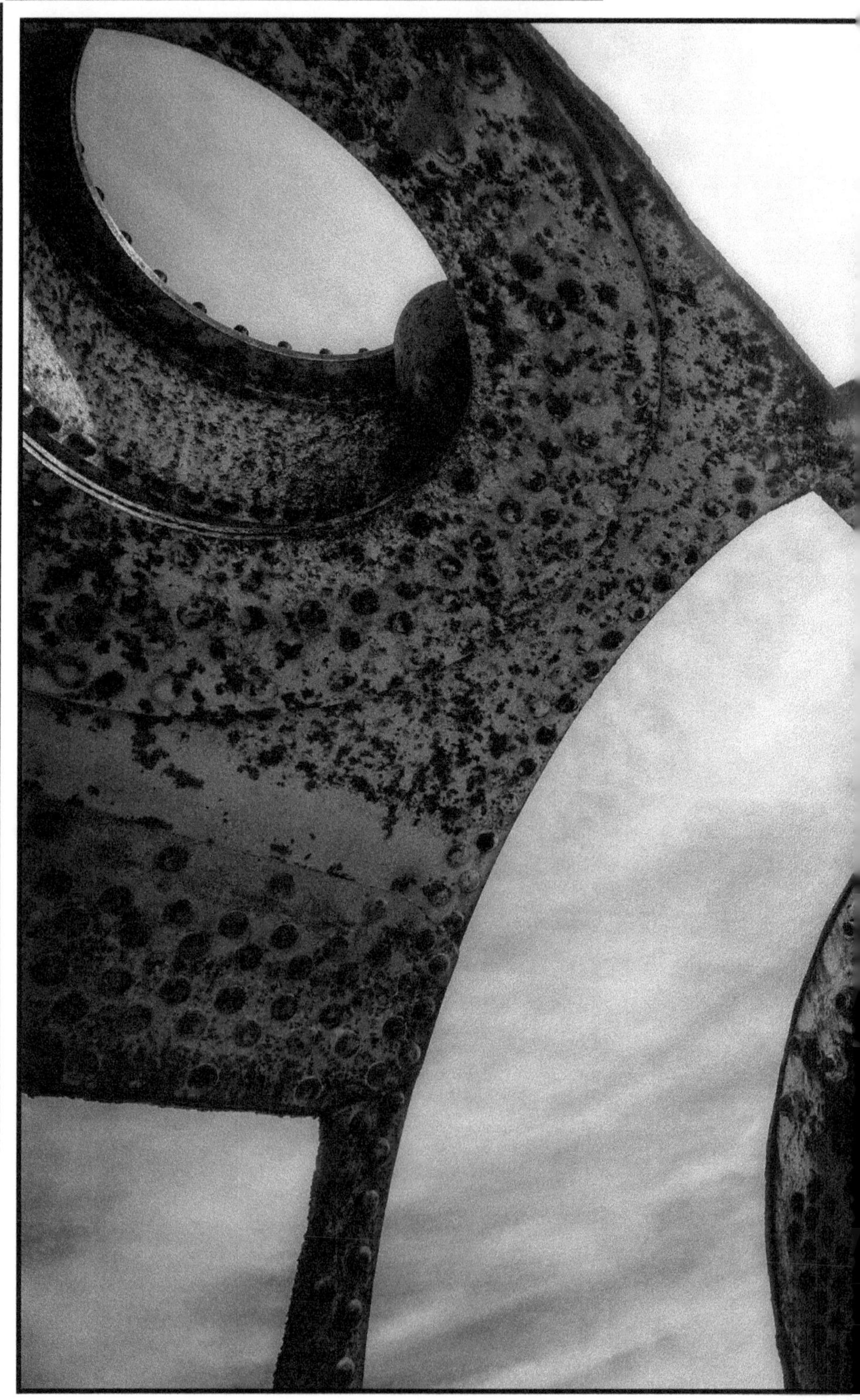

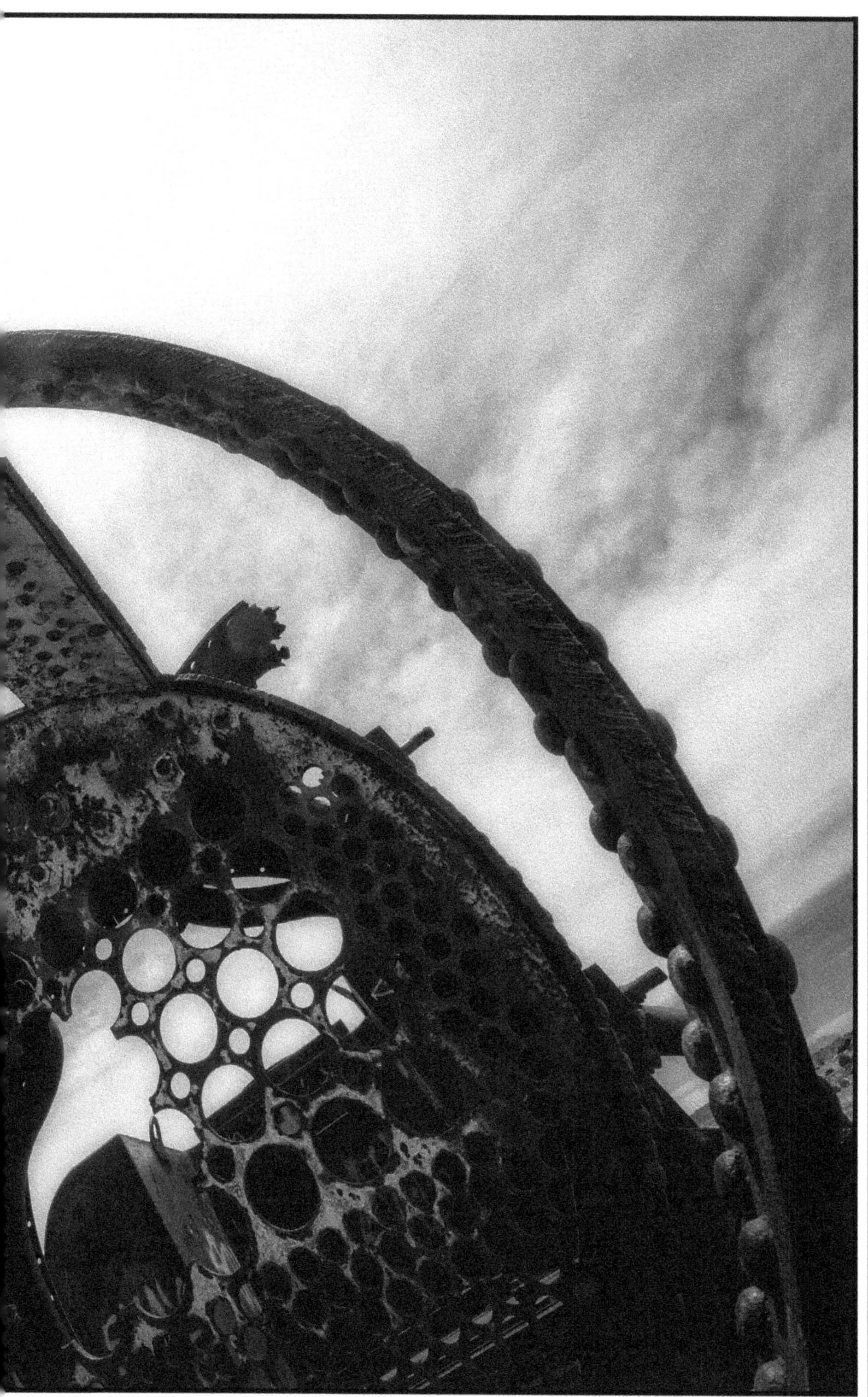

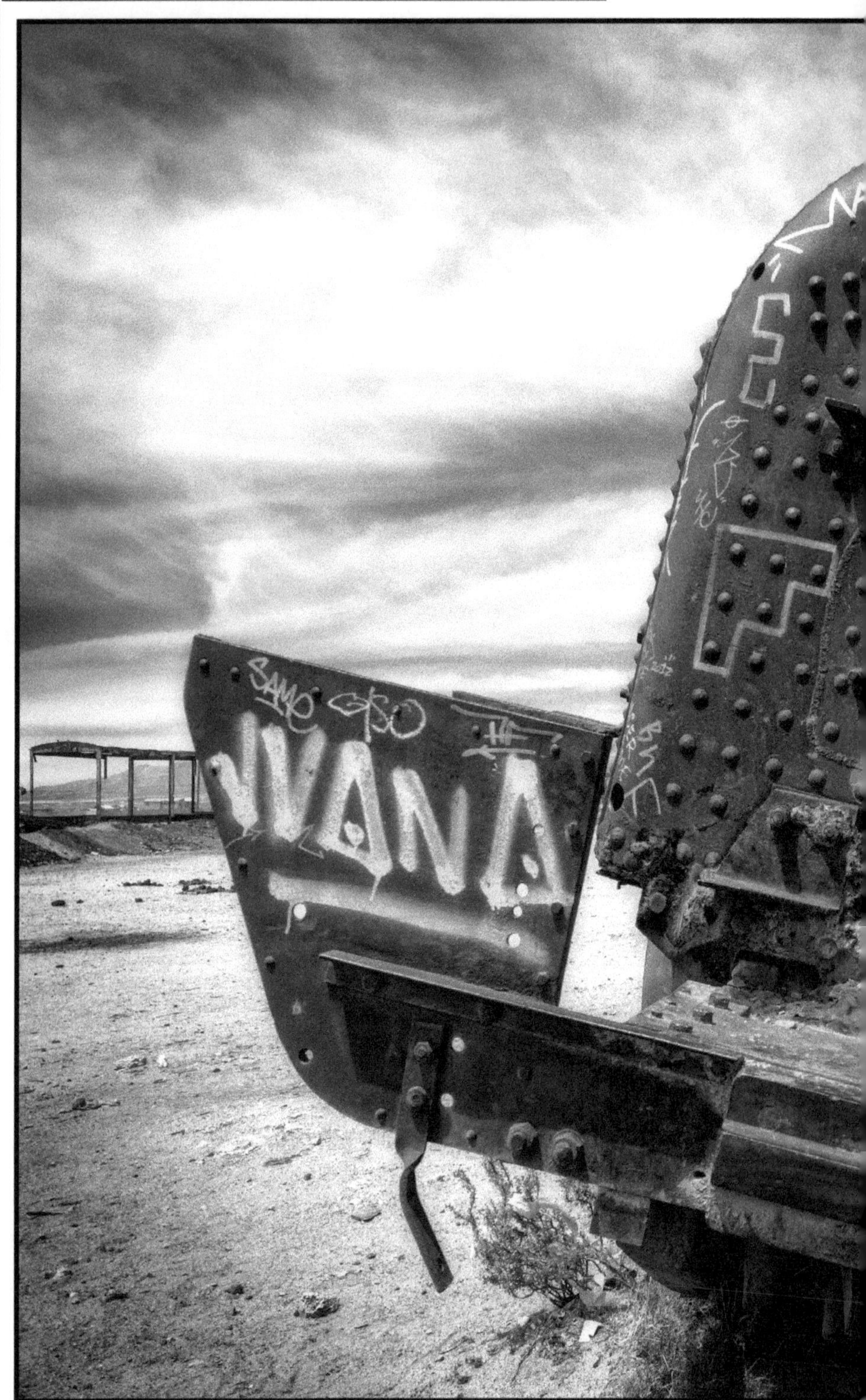
SAMO
NANA

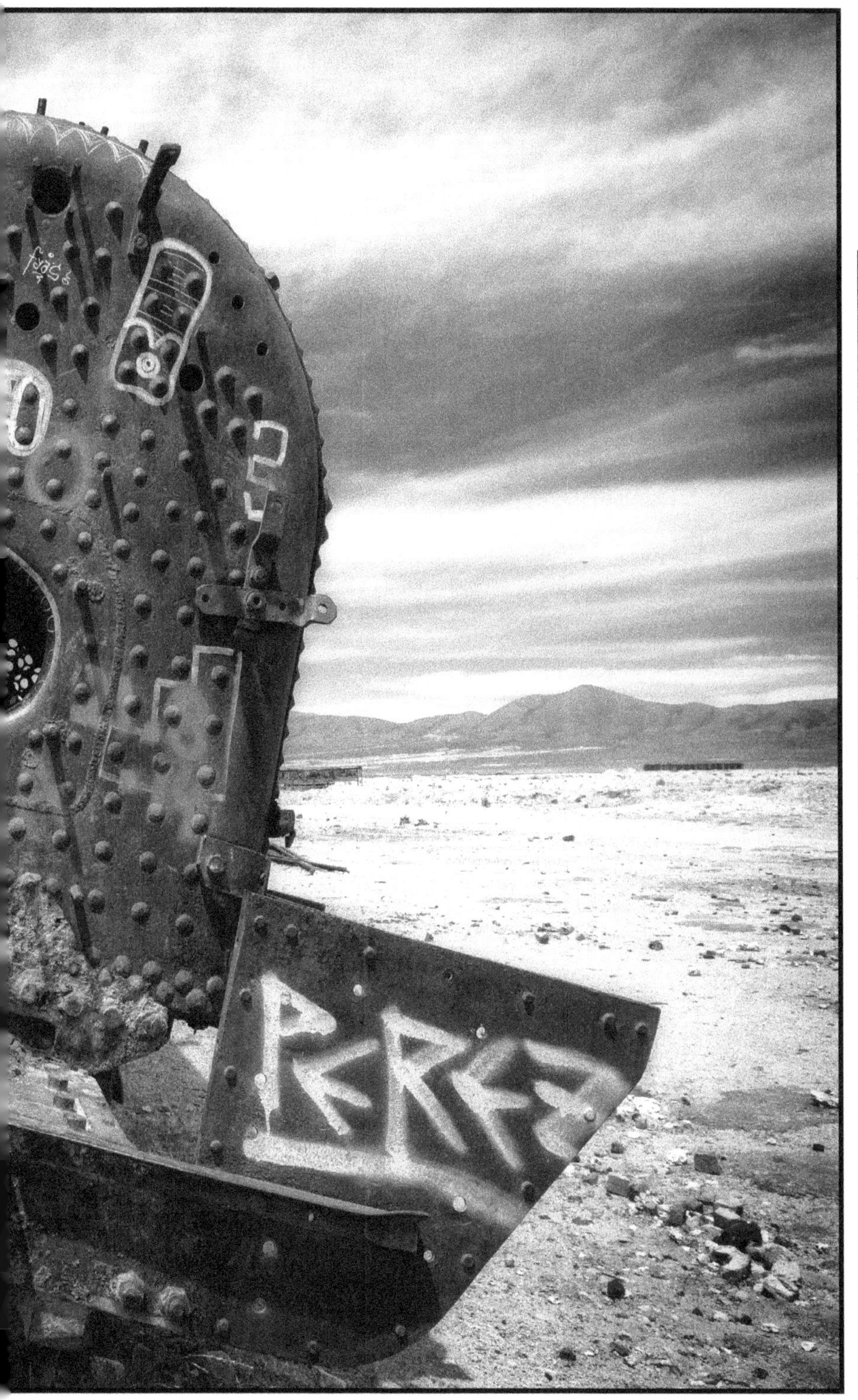

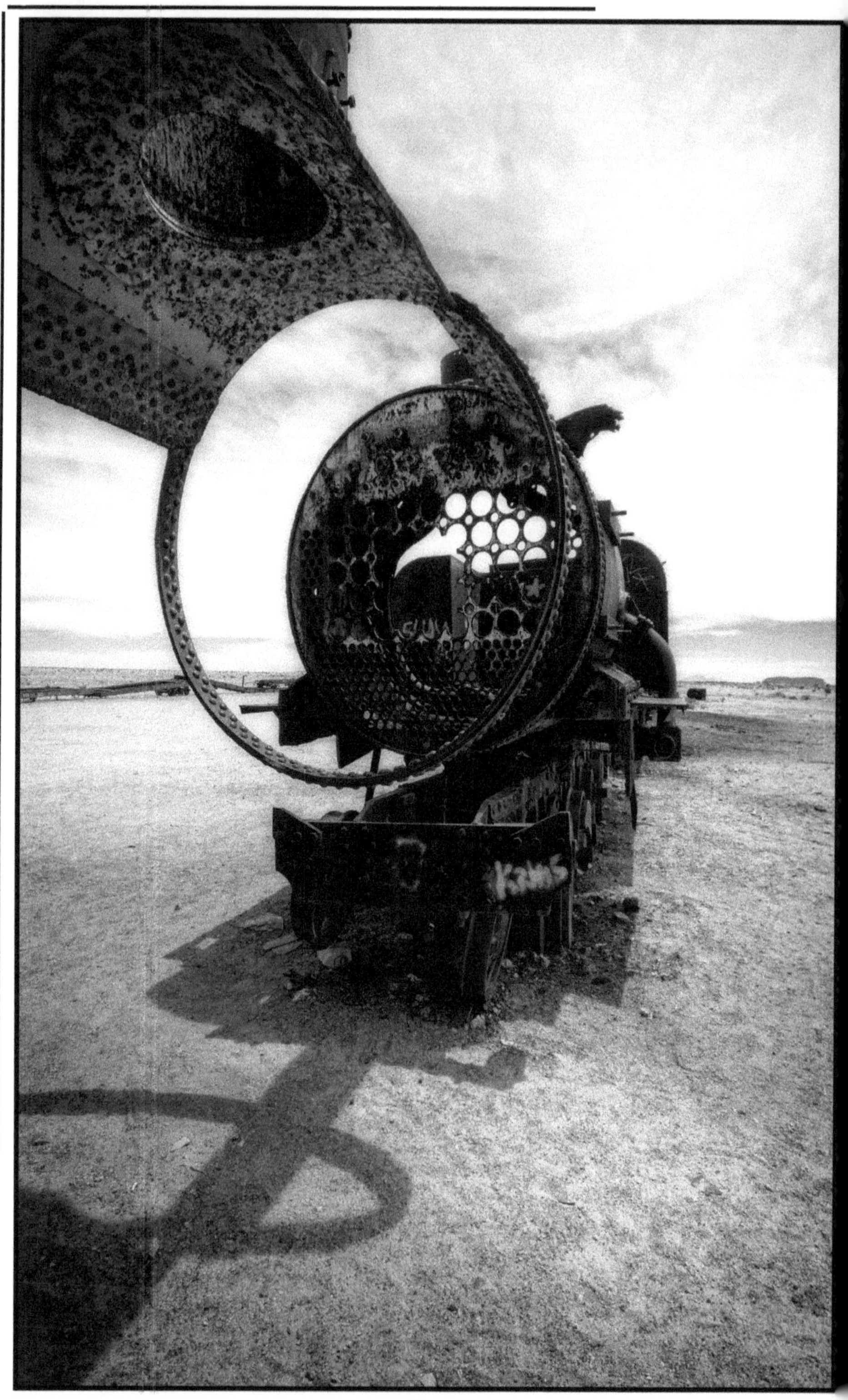

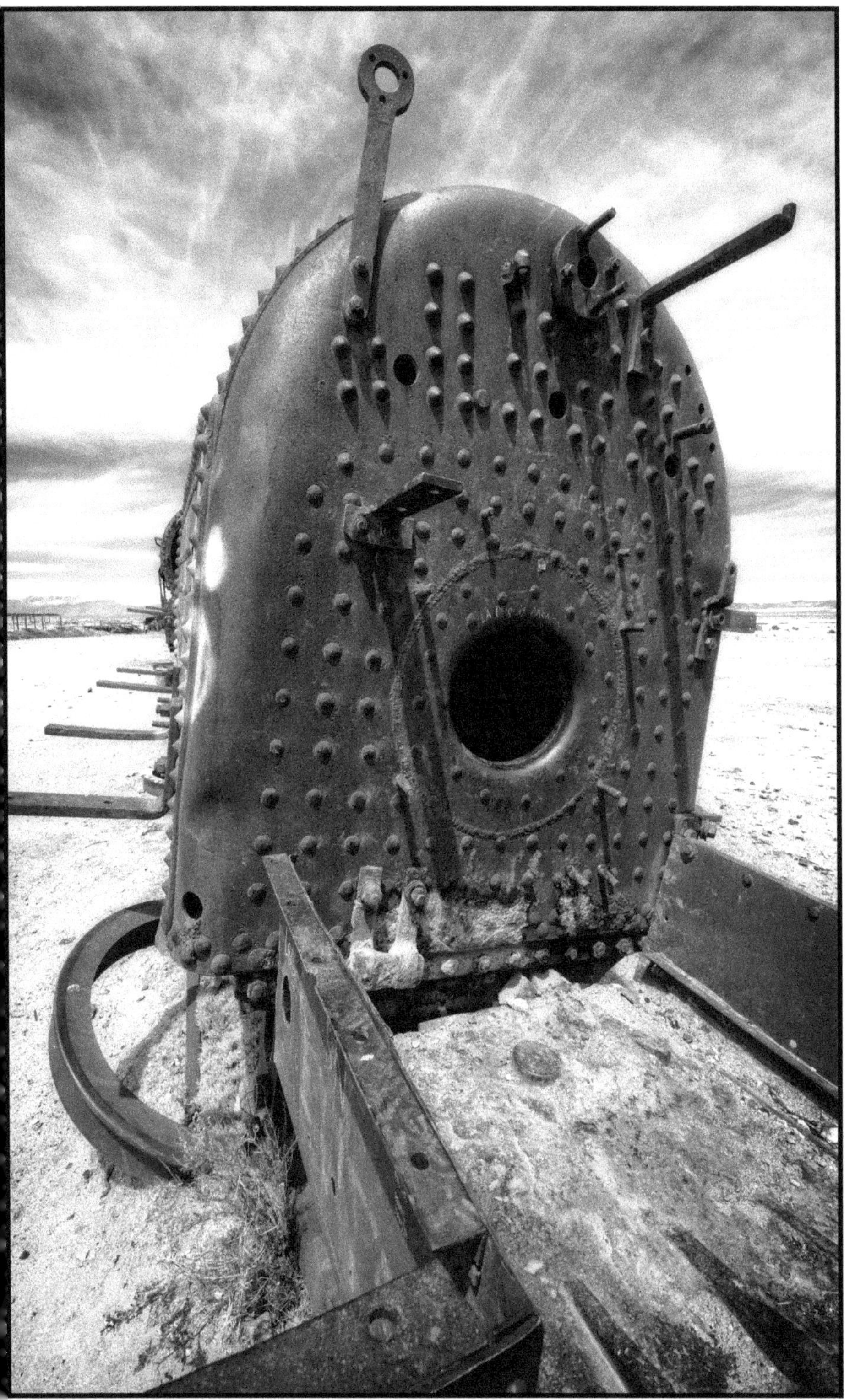

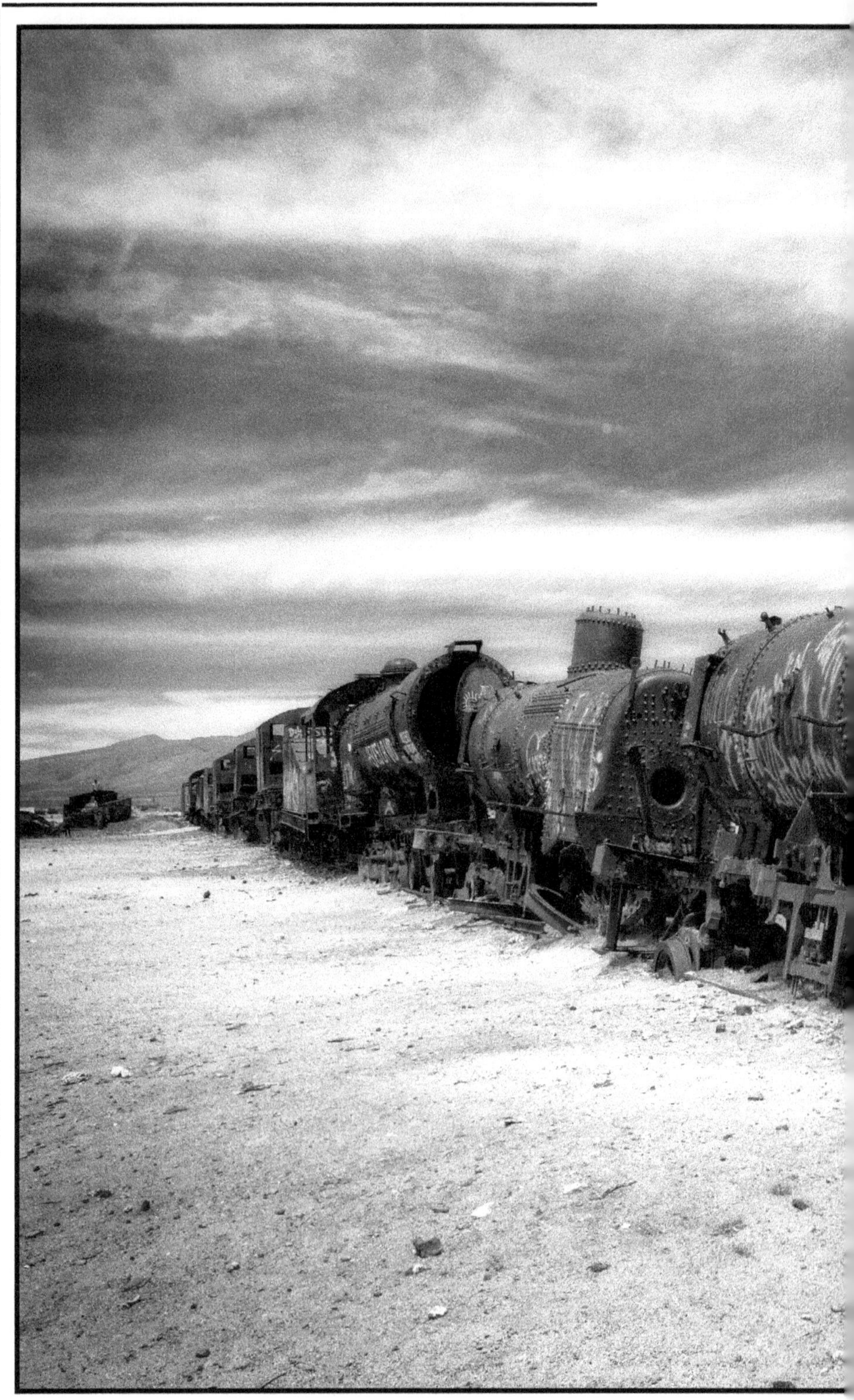

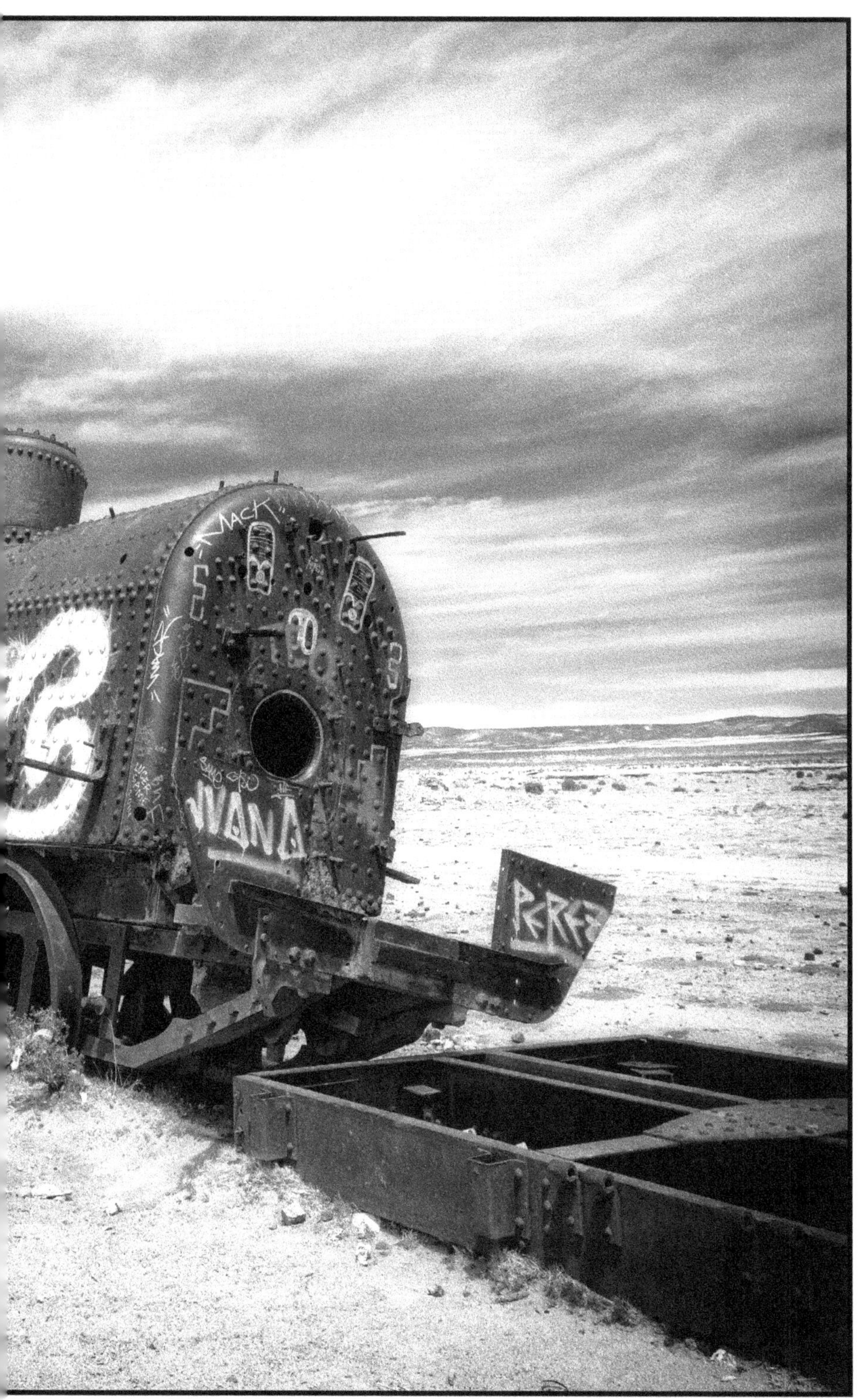

When We Left Fort Recovery

Robert McDonald

The rain was still falling, and the sky held
a sulfurous tint
to the east,
but late sunlight half-shone
onto the roads, and the water that stood
upon the roads and the unplanted fields.

In this season of deluge, the earth is too wet
to receive the corn,
and each house and outbuilding
on the farms we pass remains
an island, in a lake the color of tarnished spoons.
The highway and farm tracks glimmer

with water, hard to tell if it's merely a shimmer of wet,
or the surface of a body
that could swallow our car.
All the way back from Fort Recovery,
rows of poplars that divide the fields drip
their thin curtains of silver. A dozen cows huddle darky

at the side of a hill. When the rabbit dashes right out
in front of the car it seems impossible
for the tires to miss
or that the rabbit can swerve;
I think of the guinea hens
we saw earlier, before the storm, pom-poms

squashed red on the asphalt. But you've always been
the better driver. We remain on the road,
and the rabbit survives, disappears
in a tuft of meadow grasses. And now,
in a last reminder of sunlight, you turn in,
and the new gravel spread

across your father's driveway
pulses,
like the little ghosts
of one hundred
thousand
moons.

Plenty Some One

Chris Andrews

Actually, we haven't all been there.
Plenty never got anywhere near
the vortical mother of cities
whose natives are quick to disabuse:
"It's not as glamorous as it seems."
But being able to say that is,
and hearing it will rarely wither
the longing just to go there and breathe
what may never have been in the air.

I mutter what I want to have said
going down the staircase of the years:
We haven't all actually been there
in the slingback pumps of the door bitch
who smiles and says, "You wouldn't like it."
Some never did a charity gig.
Some went on wondering, now and then,
what it would have been like to belong
to the caste of the desirables.

They lived too. They didn't always care.
This nitrogen travelled through their lungs.
One learnt eventually, after all
the years of going down the staircase
with mounting anxiety, to stop
on the point of turning back and wait
for the end of the mental spasm
before stepping out into the street
to breathe in the live stream of sunlight.

Aghast, Innocence, and Intensity

Paul Reynolds

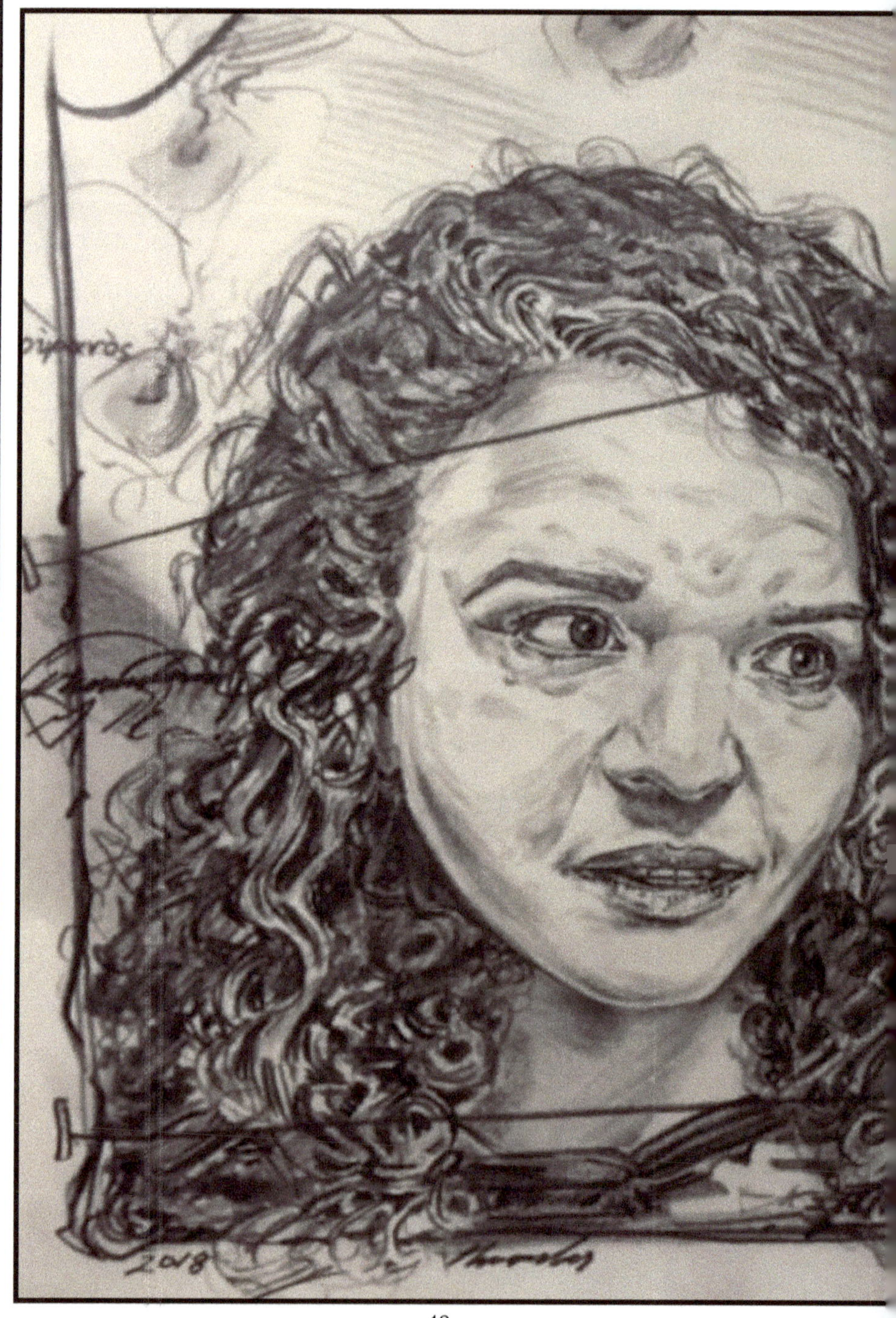

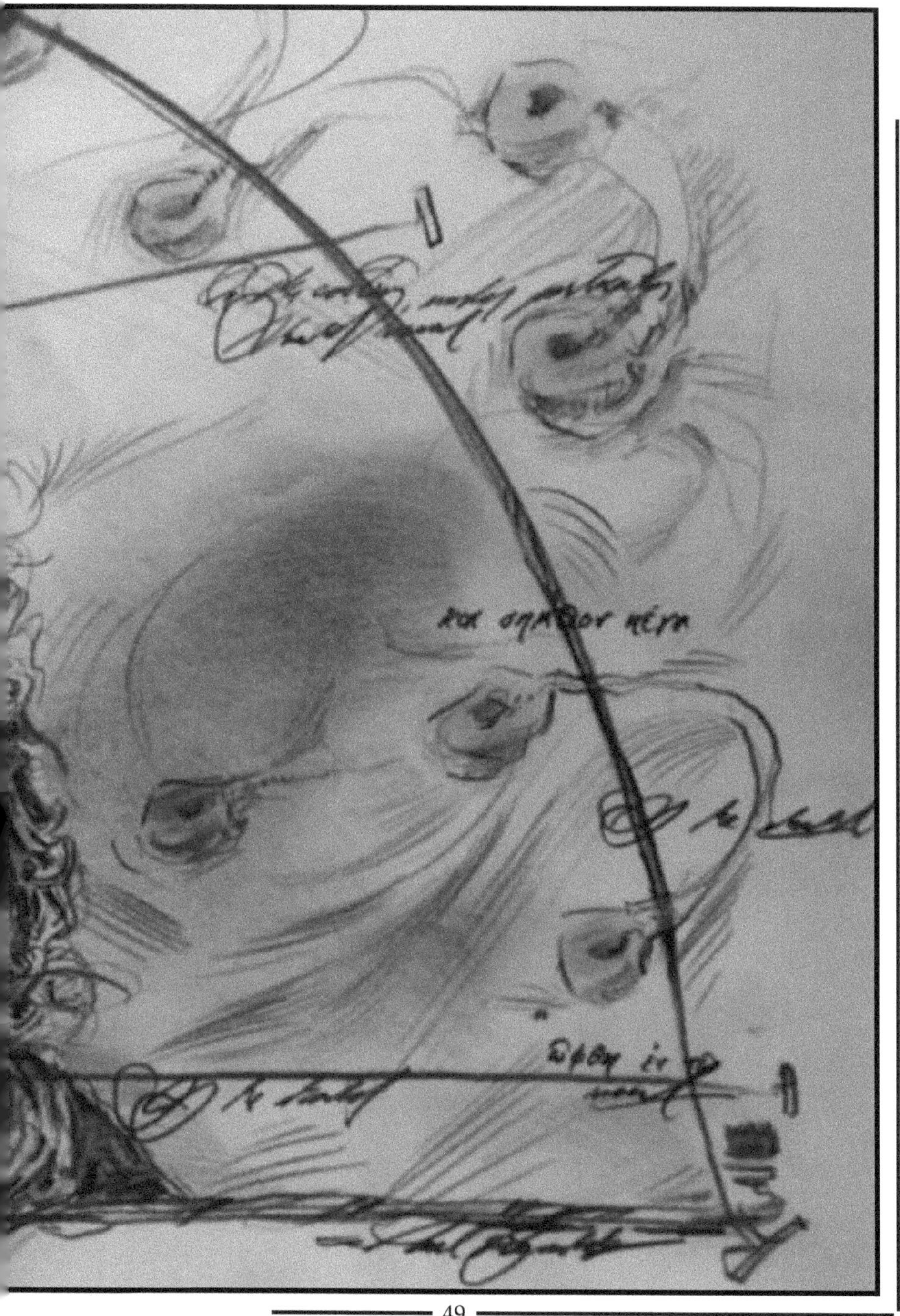

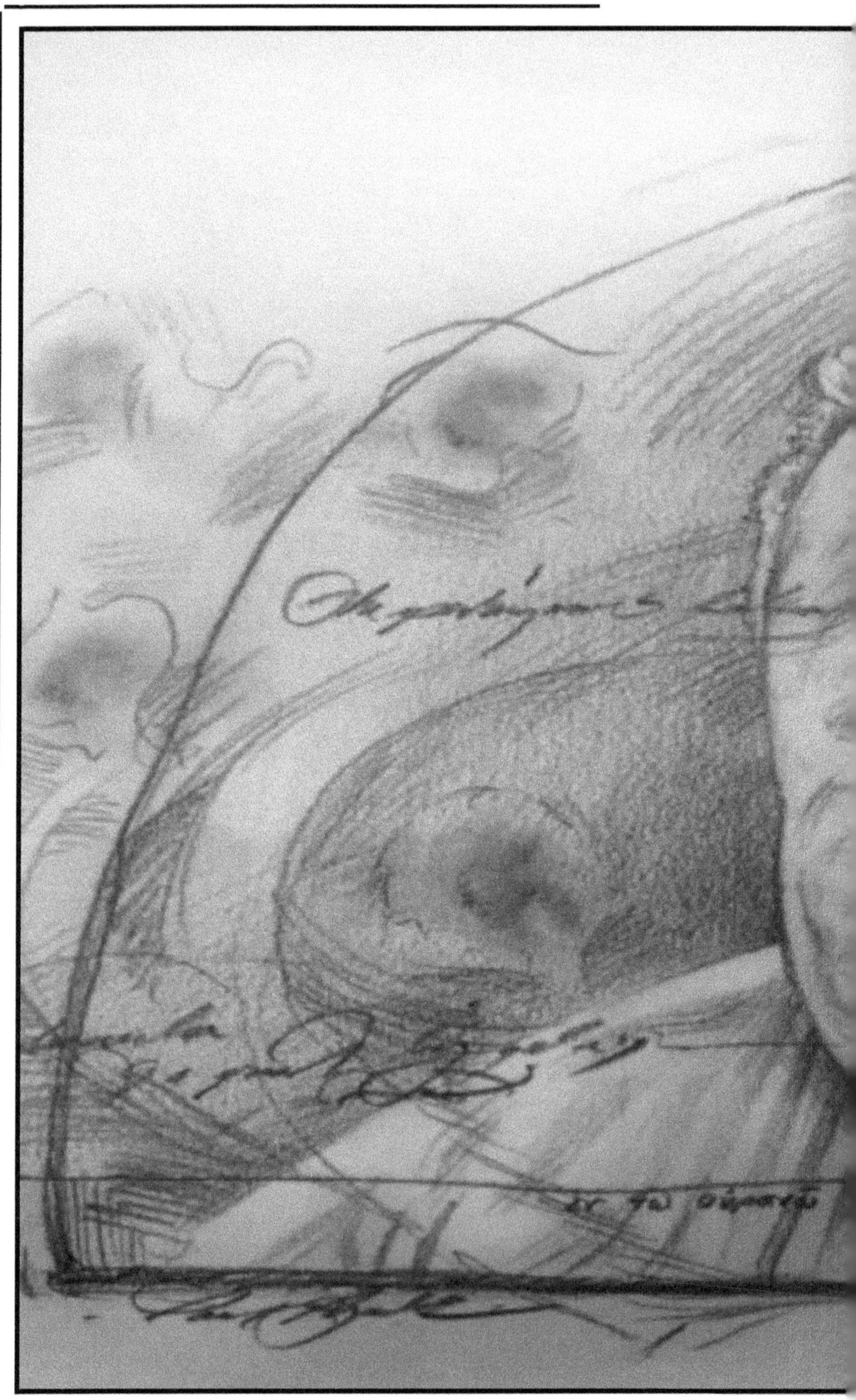

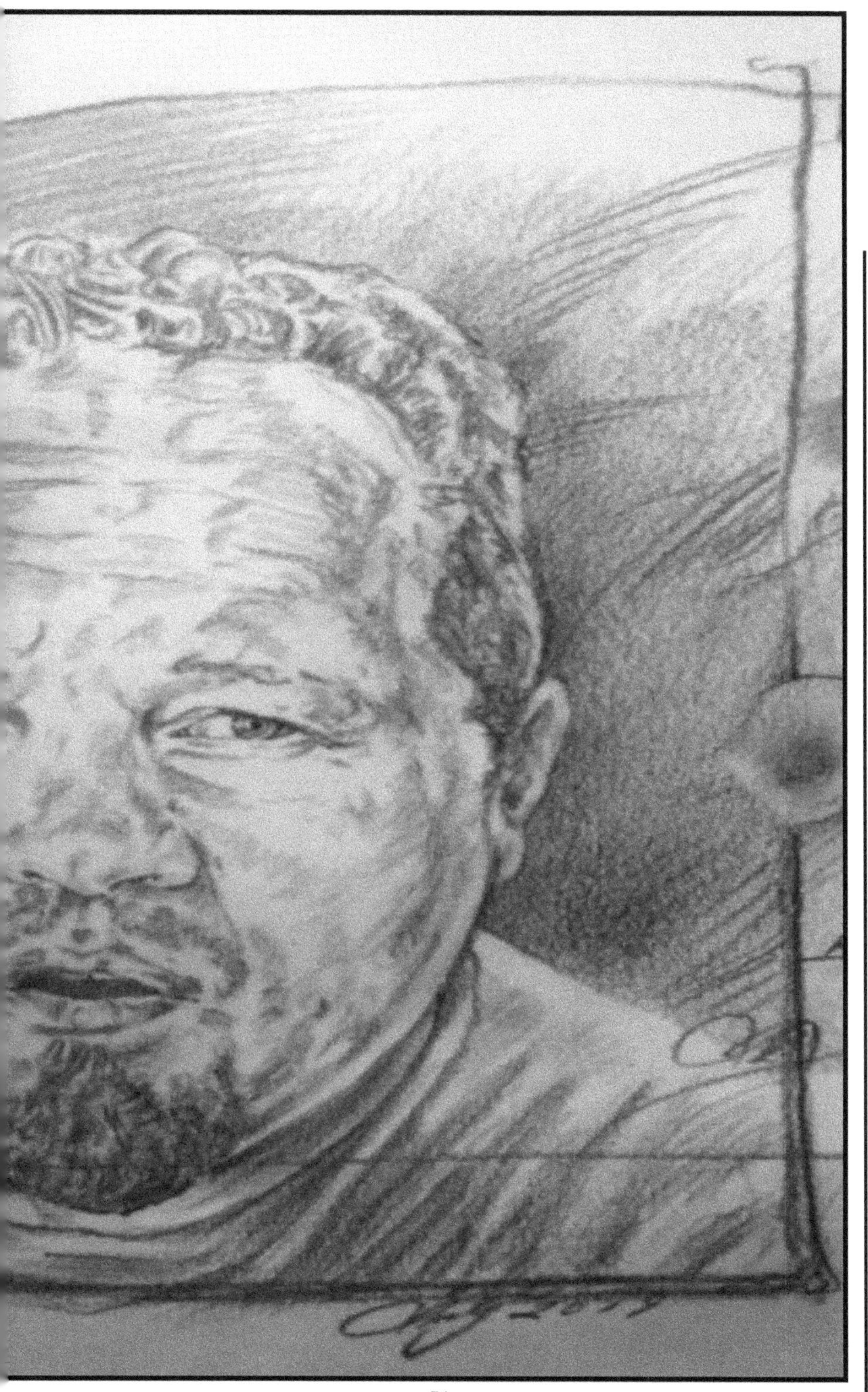

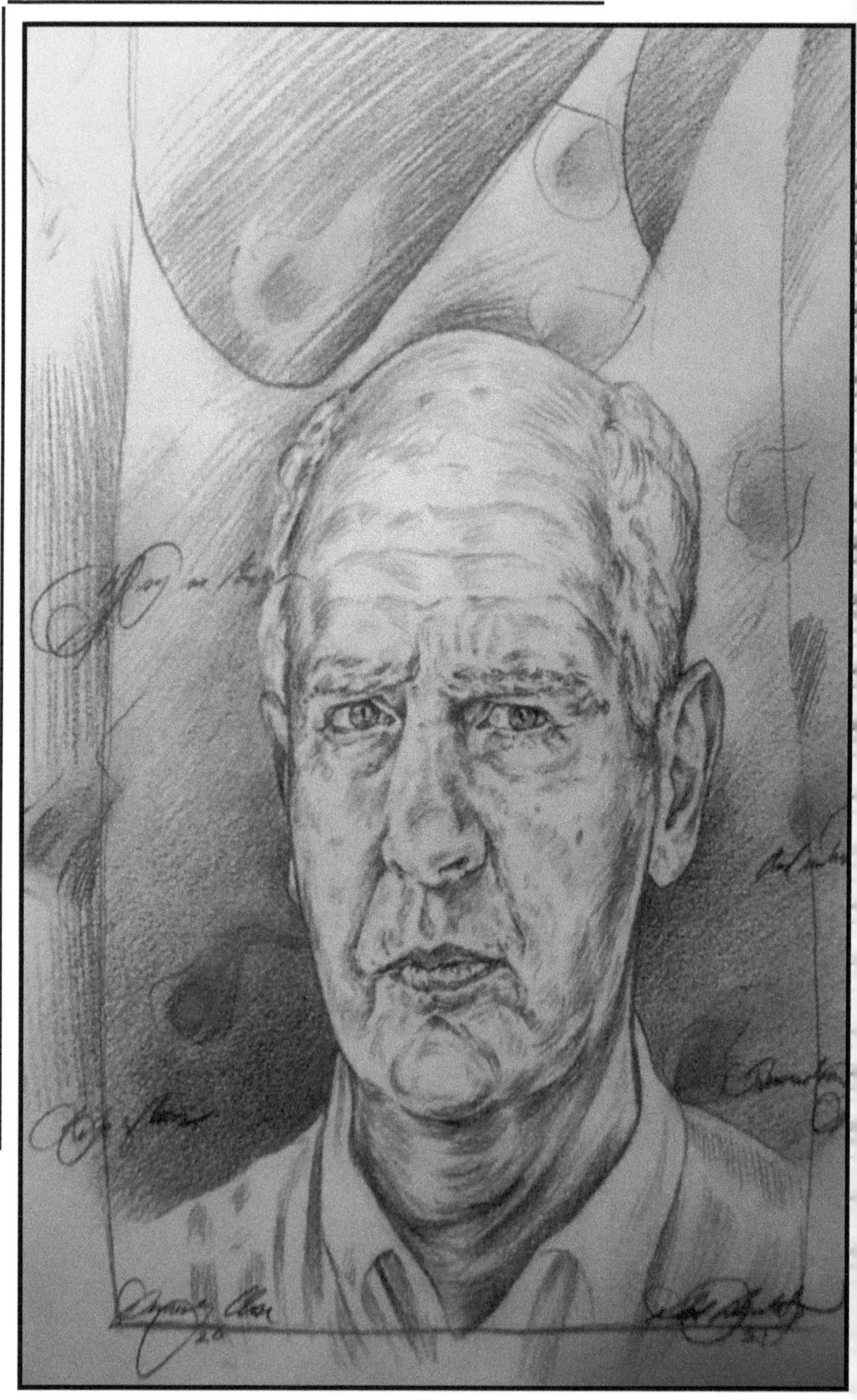

Split

Melinda Freudenberger

> "I have given my entire heart to you. If you really think you were Lot's Wife once... Now you know why I didn't turn back.. because I am the one who turned you to salt. Sorry not sorry. Much Love, Lot."

our final birth happened underneath the orange highway lights, the entire
street lit up for our arrival from nothing to nowhere, the road salted
for the two of us. this was our favorite kind of trip. i grew more sorry.
with each mile gained, my desire to be on top of kaleb sharpened my heart
into a thin, icy arrow. the killing blow would be quick. a key to being a wife
is to know how to apologize with your body. *pull over,* i say and i turn

toward him. it's so easy to fall in love with the way he hurt me. i turn
to stone at the sound of his voice, stiffen up into grieving postures of entire
generations of women before me. the necklace he asked me to be his wife
with at my throat, the cigarettes he gifted me now as vital to me as salt.
we were young. awake till the dawn, the sky split open to reveal a heart
so raw, throbbing pink and orange split with a blue, a wet banner of sorry

eating up our familiar views. kaleb, singing to me and off-key suddenly: *sorry,*
he mumbled. one signature of a conor oberst song is an emotional turn—
in "lua," oberst upends an empathetic refrain: *i know you have a heavy heart,*
i can feel it when we kiss with the disarming clarity of the daytime, an entire
connection built on ignorance. *you can count on me to split,* oberst sings. salt
is essential for preservation. sometimes i imagine lot returning to his wife

in a moment of remembrance, scraping a little bit of salt from his wife's
body—out of grief or a selfish need? can it be both? as kaleb said sorry
through his songs, i lifted my finger to the light. the tip of it was salt;
i flicked it off onto the floor. you know how the body runs out, turns
bitter. *what is simple in the moonlight by the morning never is*—entirely
true, my two men lament and, yes, they were talking of me and my heart

filled with demands: an exhausting, needy machine that cinched his heart
so perfectly—*tighter,* i commanded, *and tighter*—he needed me as his wife.
i am desperate to name you in front of the world. don't you remember entire
years of our lives delineated by your excuses? it was not enough to say sorry.
like you had predicted: language had failed us. today i woke up and turned
to my window and, rustling underneath my foot, a dead bee crumbled like salt:

its striped torso split into fourths, stinger wound tight in its final effort—the salt
of the earth always returns, i am reminded. i thought of you. i thought of your heart

at the end of the world. i thought of riding you in the front seat of your car, turning
my head just enough to catch the moon from the window. another key to being a wife
is to understand when it is finished—finding the strength not to feel sorry
for the love lost but instead taking a final picture: the sweat on his brow, his entire

body shaking beneath me, eyes lidded and glittering. would a body be so entirely
mine ever again? it was a risk i had to take—an orgasm was the only sorry
i knew. *baby,* he whispered into me for a final time, *baby, my baby, my wife.*

Ahistorical

Kirsten Hemmy

It offends to see it, "the Golden Age," as though Muslims
ourselves have let it slip away, as if it weren't stolen & starved

by democracies & other imperial bodies, suffocated by water
shortages & silenced by bullets to be retold in textbooks.

"Muslim women at *that* time participated in all fields of life,"
says National Geographic, pointing italicized implication

that now they somehow do not. (My doctor, bank manager,
boss & her boss are all participatory.) How you see us &

who we are are at odds—stranger upon stranger upon
bewildered family member asks me who made me put this scarf

on, prostrate on this rug. No one I say, or me. I did. The number
of times patriarchy has failed, set out to destroy me & nearly

succeeded. When we choose for ourselves—anything—some man
inevitably thinks it's about men. Why can't it be true that I harnessed

my own tattered ordinary & built it into the extraordinary I am now?
My aesthetic is not new & is thanks to no man. It is golden. Aged.

We've been rebirthing ourselves for thousands of suns, pulling
light into the wounds of our everywhere. "During Muslim civilization,

numerous women excelled" rings you don't know us or see us past
our visible but personal choices atop your historical underestimations.

Dreaming

Diamante Lavendar

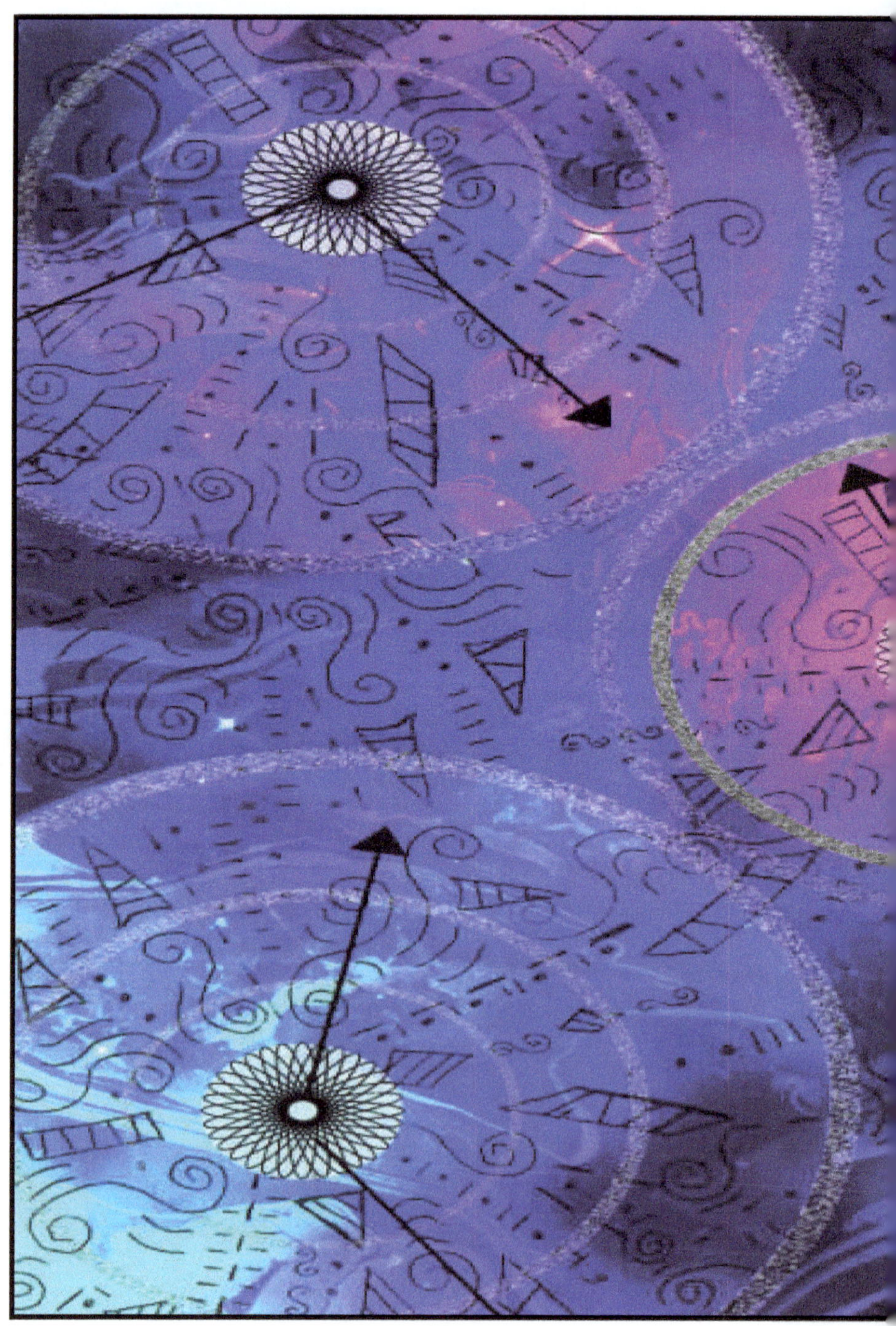

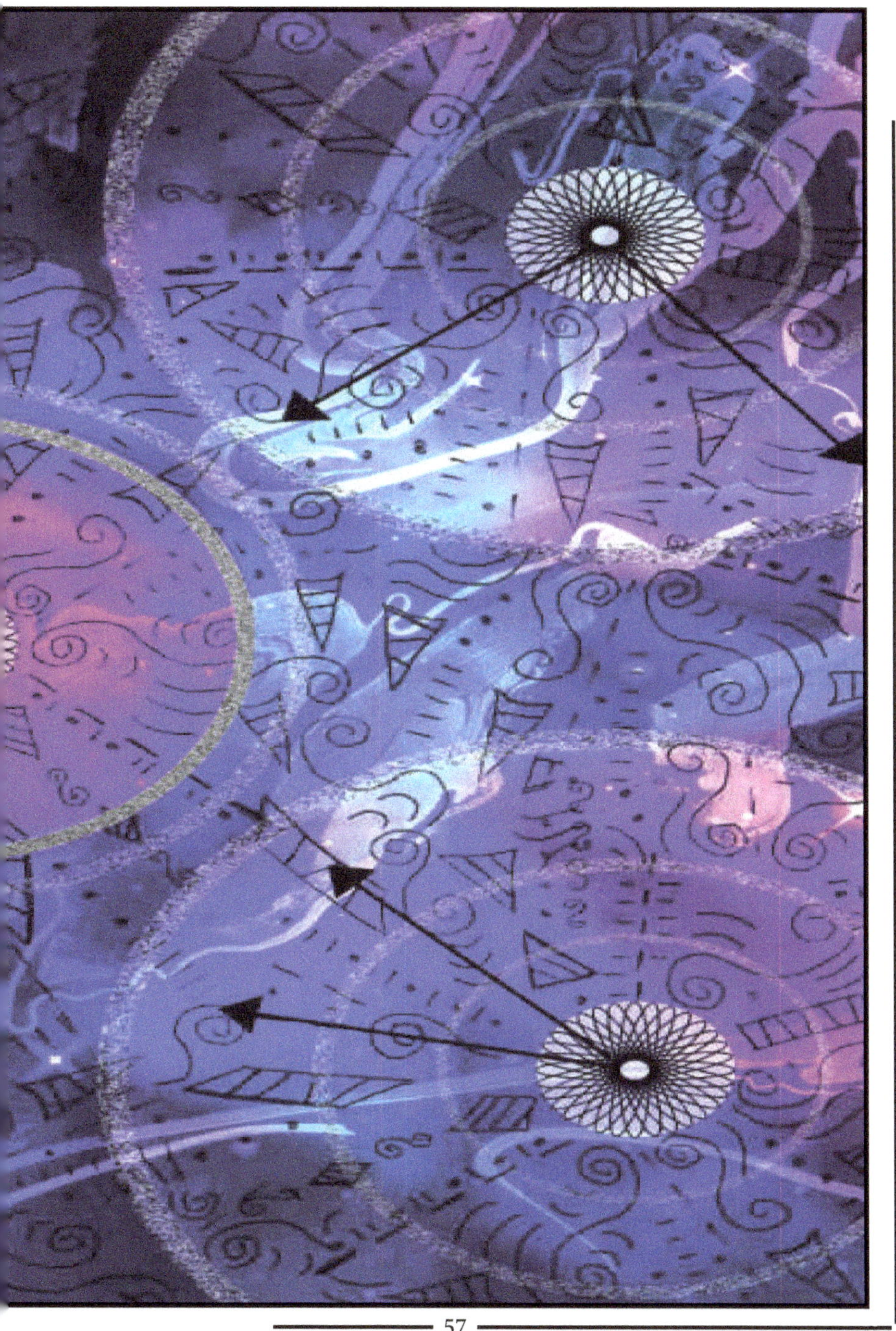

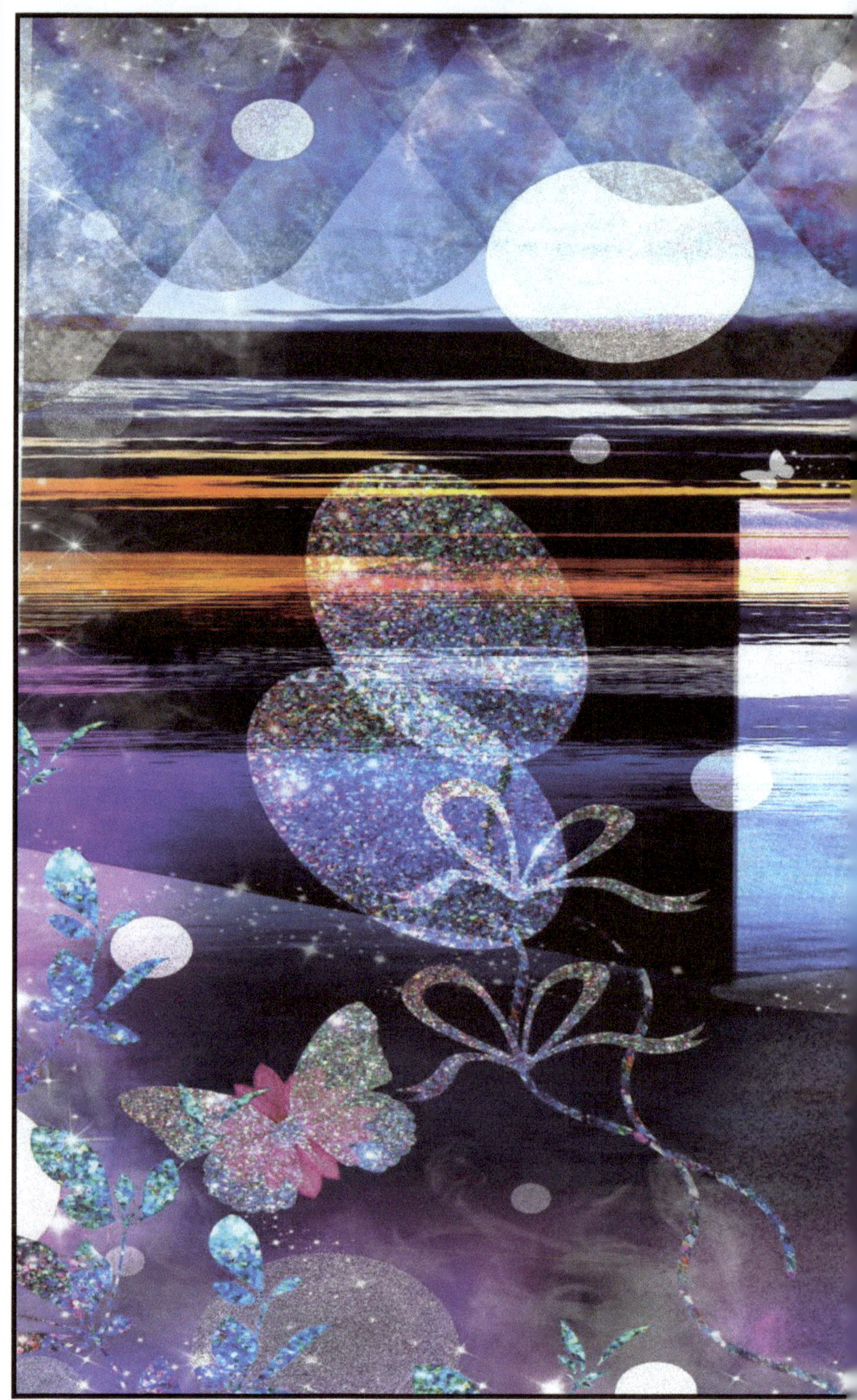

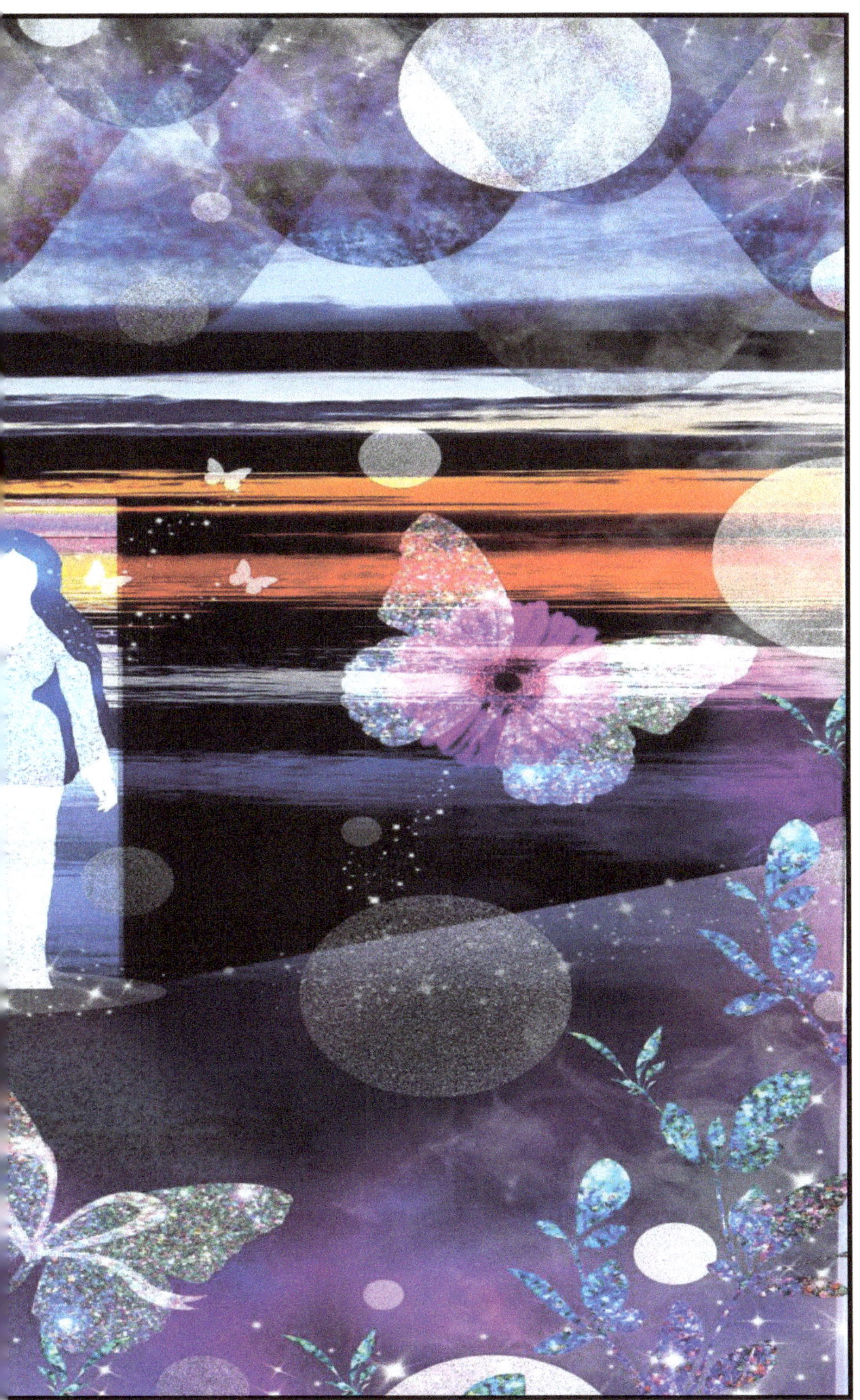

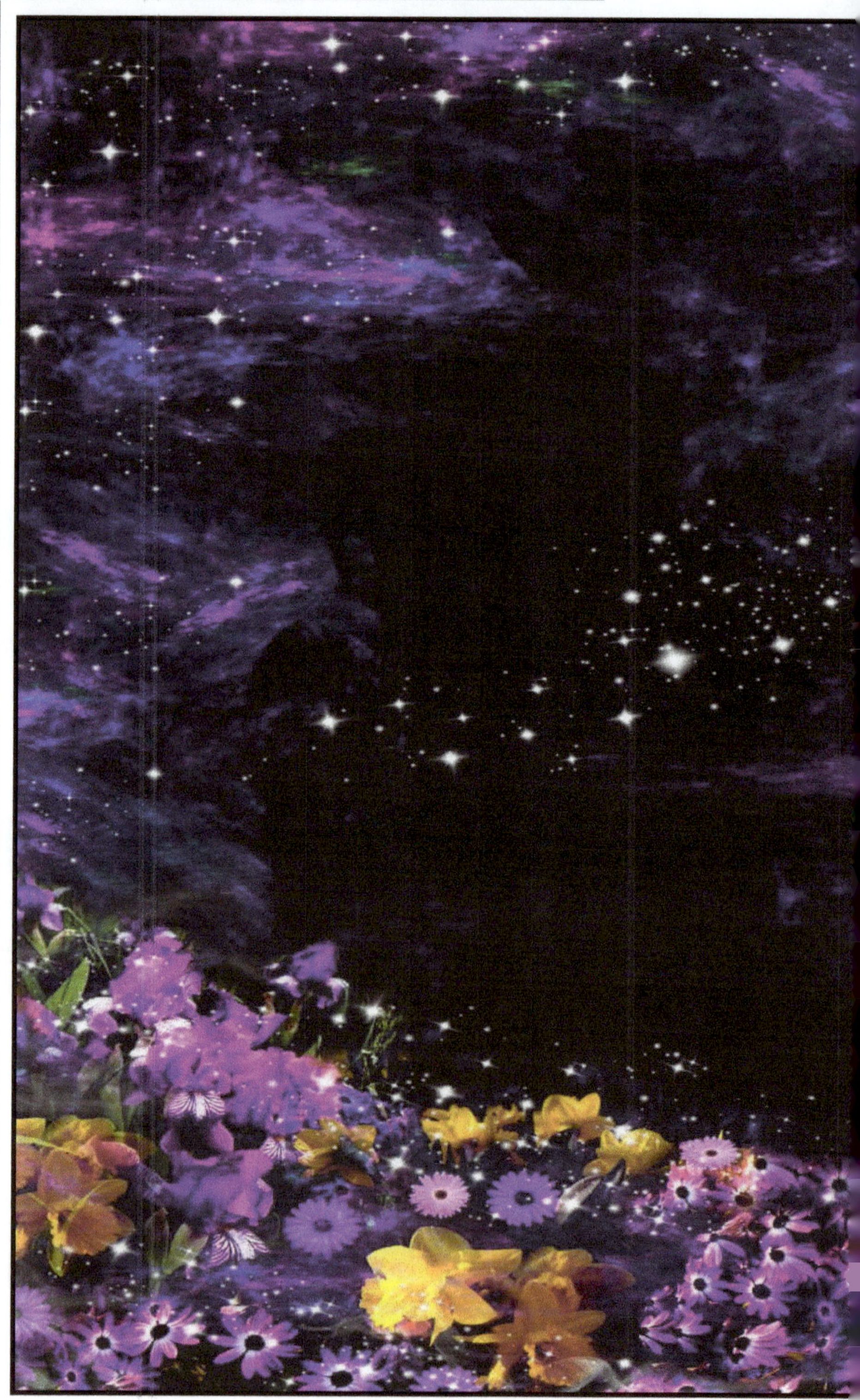

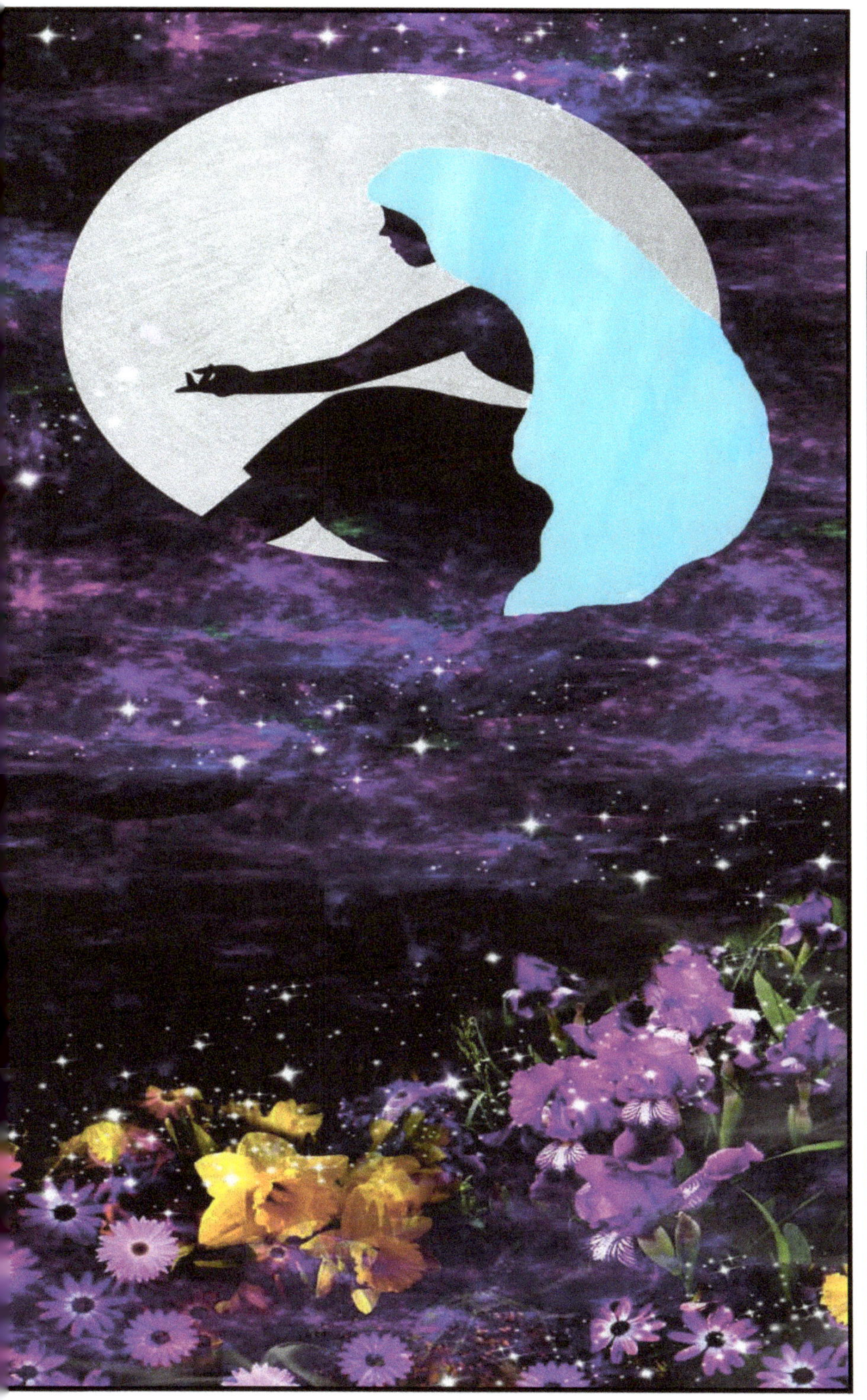

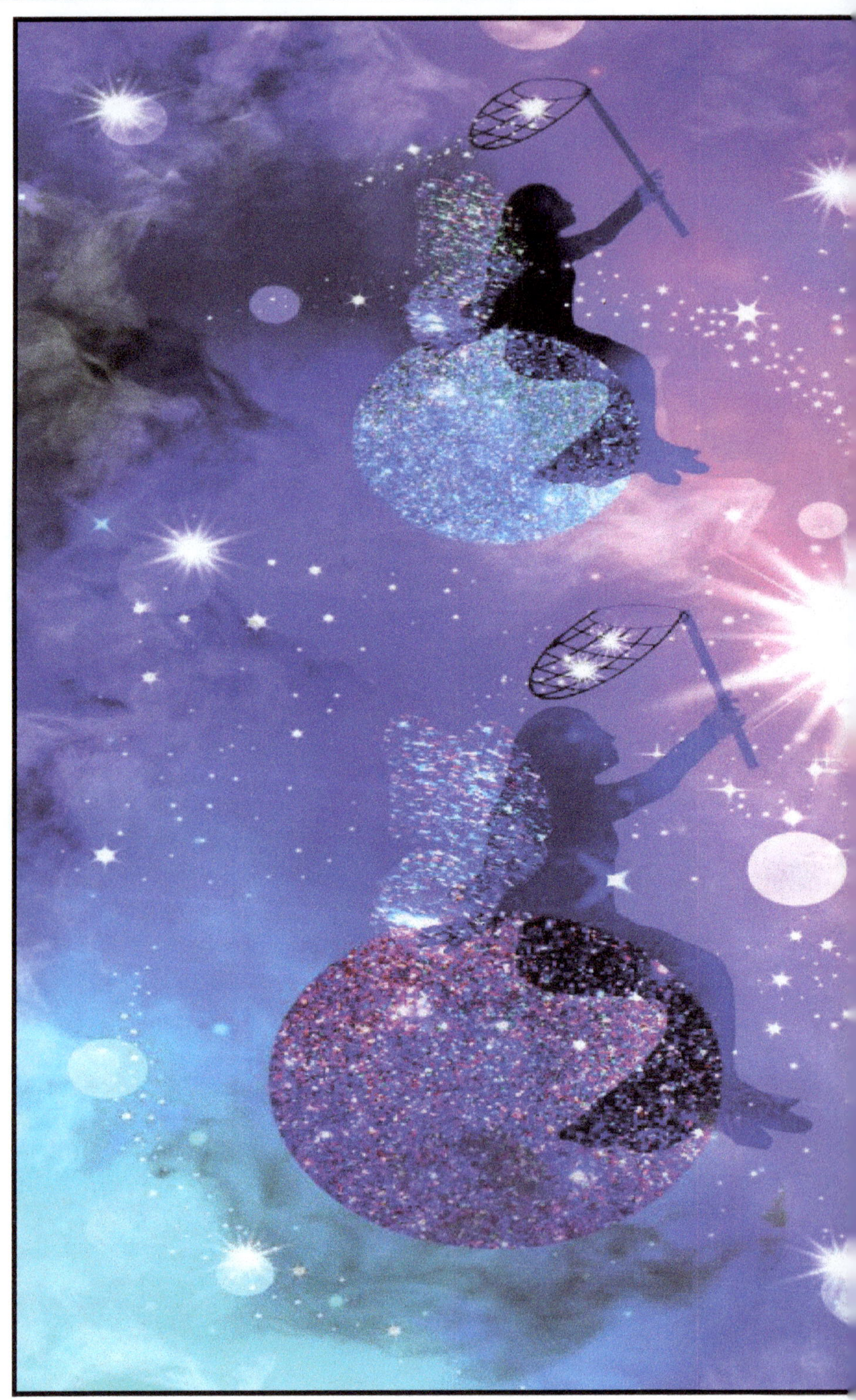

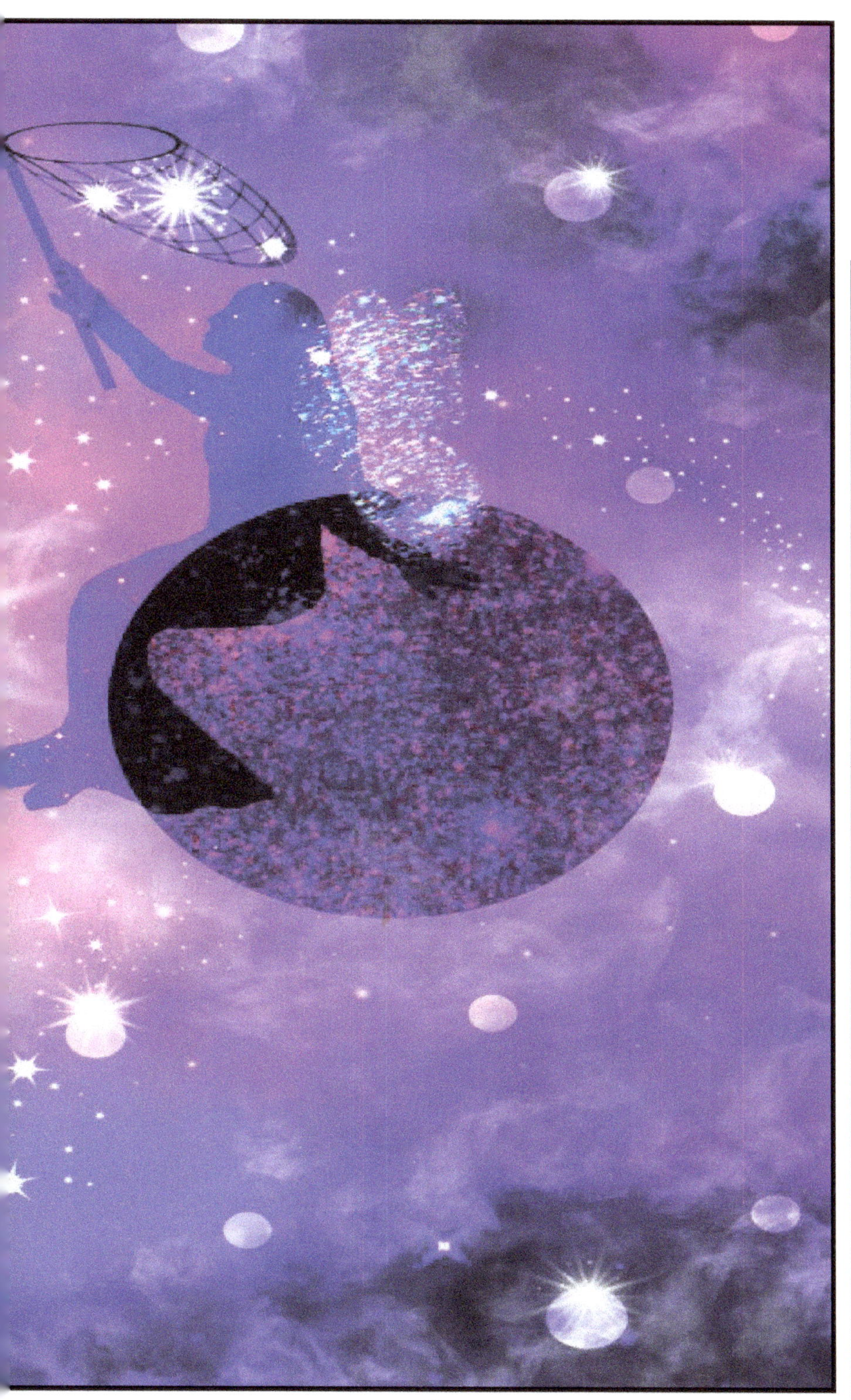

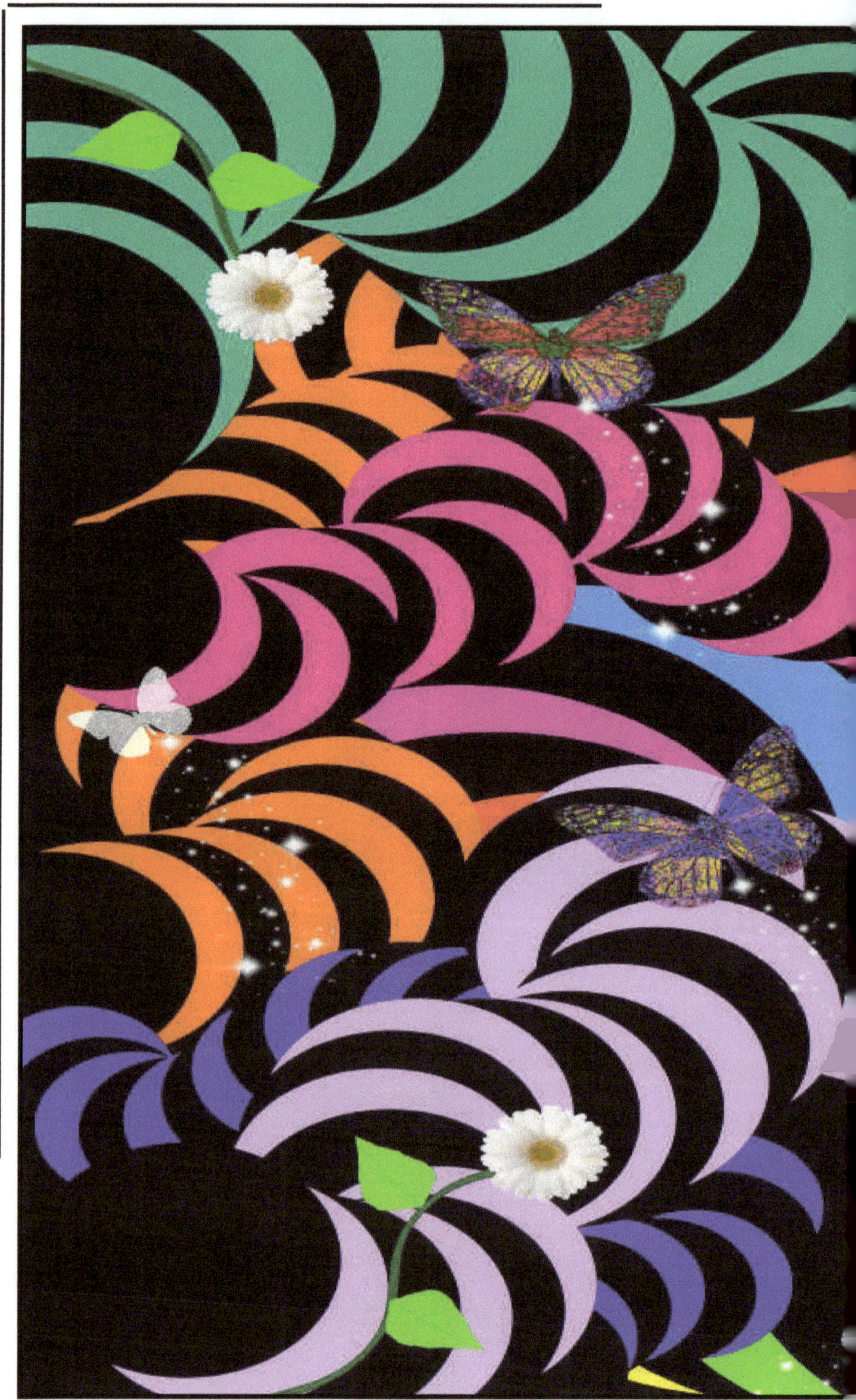

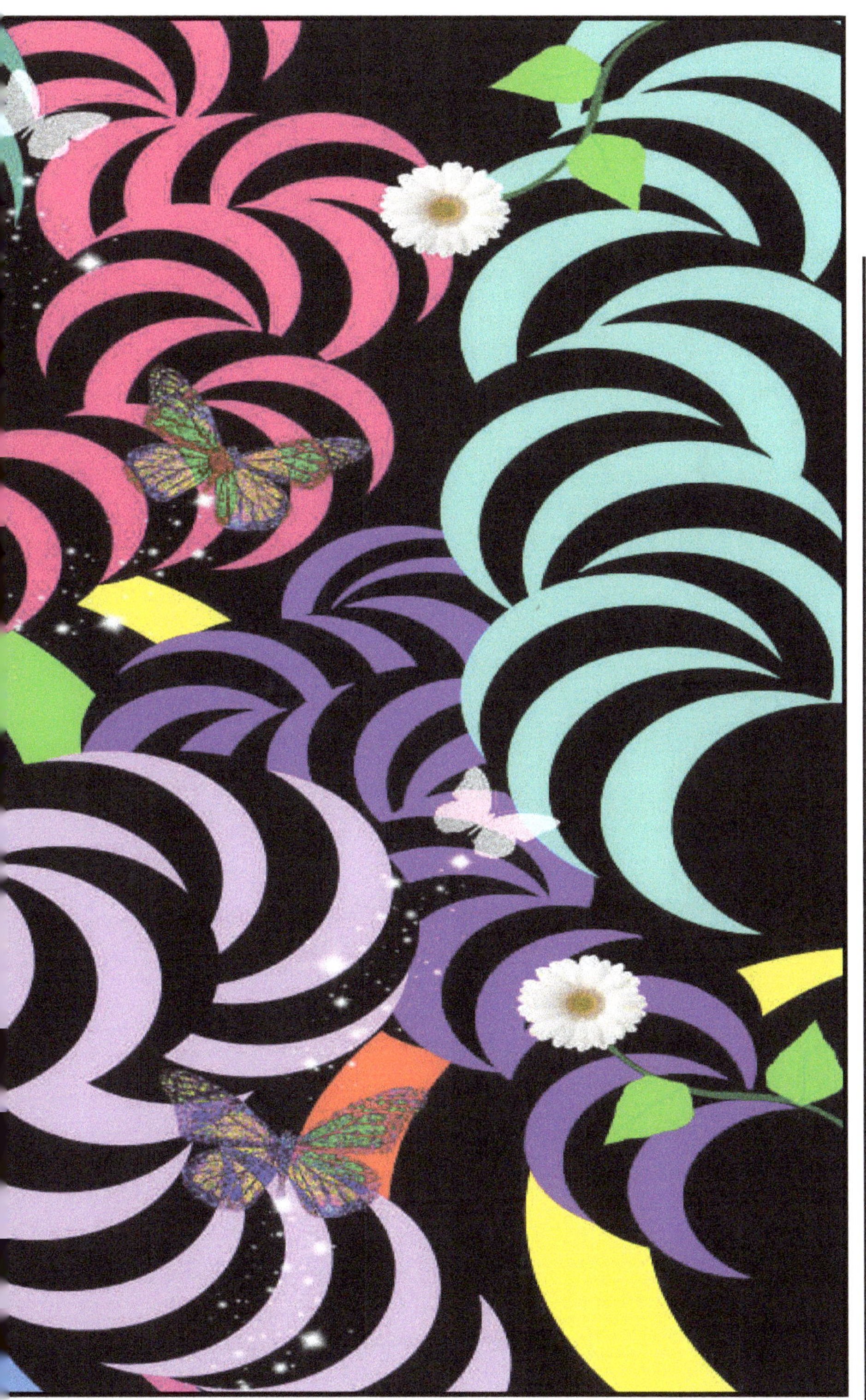

ACT Practice Test in the Time of COVID

Candice Kelsey

<u>Directions</u>: Select the answer choice that best conveys the disappointment you are feeling, creates the most grammatically correct sentiment for your crushed dreams, or is the most consistent with the frustration and fear you are experiencing. If you decide that your pre-pandemic way of life was more fulfilling, you may select NO CHANGE. Please note that this selection is rarely —if ever—a possible answer and often leads to a lower score. You may also find questions will arise from frequent and often conflicting announcements by various government officials. For these questions, decide which response best accomplishes the ultimate goal of maintaining your mental health while also watching your sports season slip away, your commencement ceremony crumble, or your parents' paychecks disappear. After you've selected the best choice, fill in the corresponding oval in your answer grid with the same care you mask your nose and mouth, being careful not to allow your imagination to confuse the ABCDEs with COVIDs or tiny rows of a thousand new graves. For some questions, you'll need to find the courage and resolve to know there are no easy answers—especially now. Finally, be sure you have enough information to determine that the correct answer choice always involves *gentleness, patience, and hope.* NOW GO ON TO THE NEXT PAGE.

Exercise I: Definitions

Alex Mepham

Expected time: 05 minutes

Write your answers next to each sentence. This is independent work. **DO NOT** discuss with anyone else.

Keywords: damp, drenched, moist, saturated, soaked, sodden, wet.

1. The feel of linen after a washing machine cycle: _______________
2. The rocks as the tide recedes: _______________
3. Your jeans when you return from a walk with unforecasted rain: _______________
4. A sponge so filled with water that the slightest touch oozes its contents: _________
5. When you press against your grandmother's fruitcake and the sugar residue remains on your finger: _______________
6. Your jeans when you return from a walk after falling in the lake: _______________
7. The coffee filter once the water has seeped through, the paper now cold: _______________

Answers will be shared at the beginning of next week's class.

Surrealism

Chris Boyko

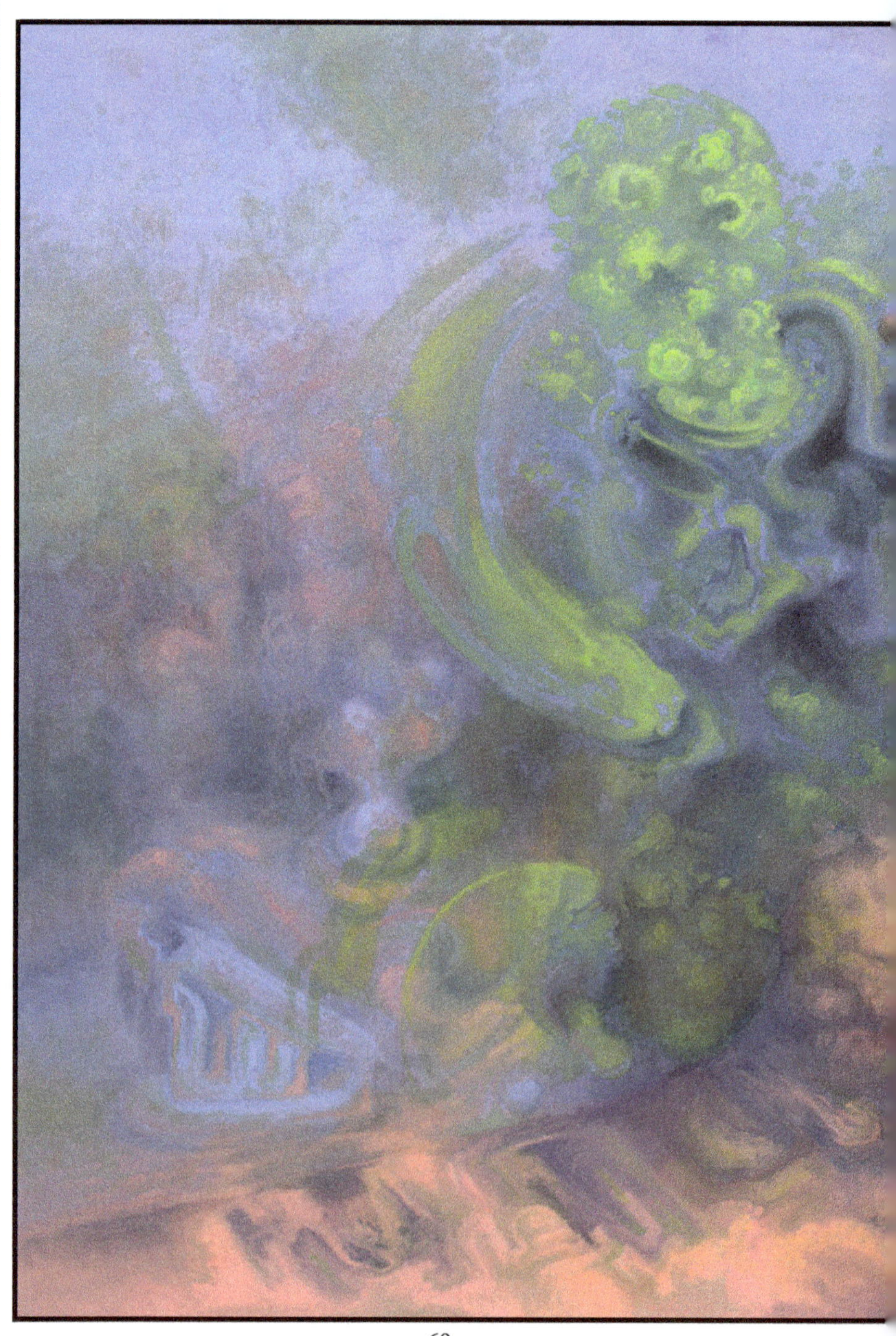

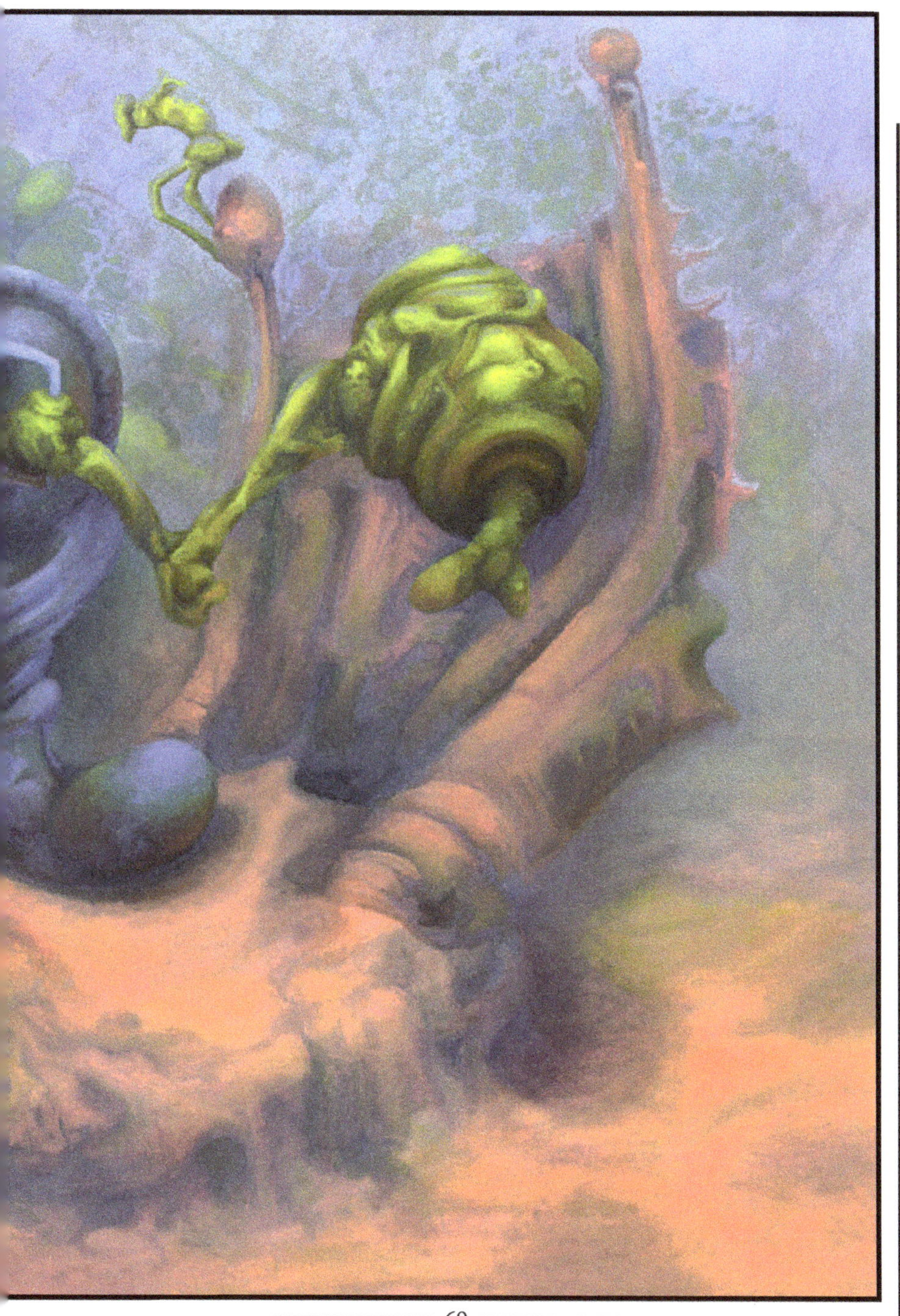

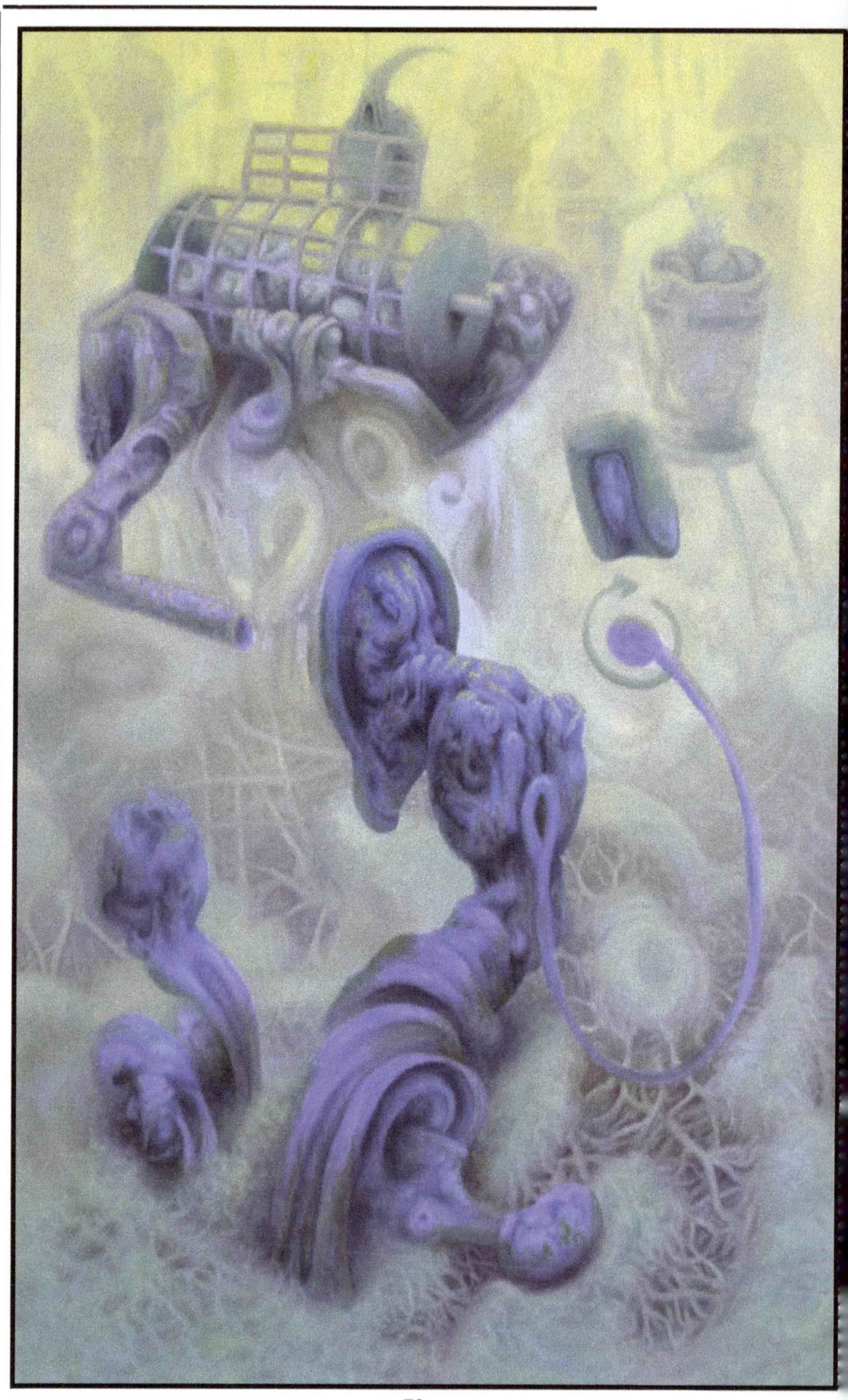

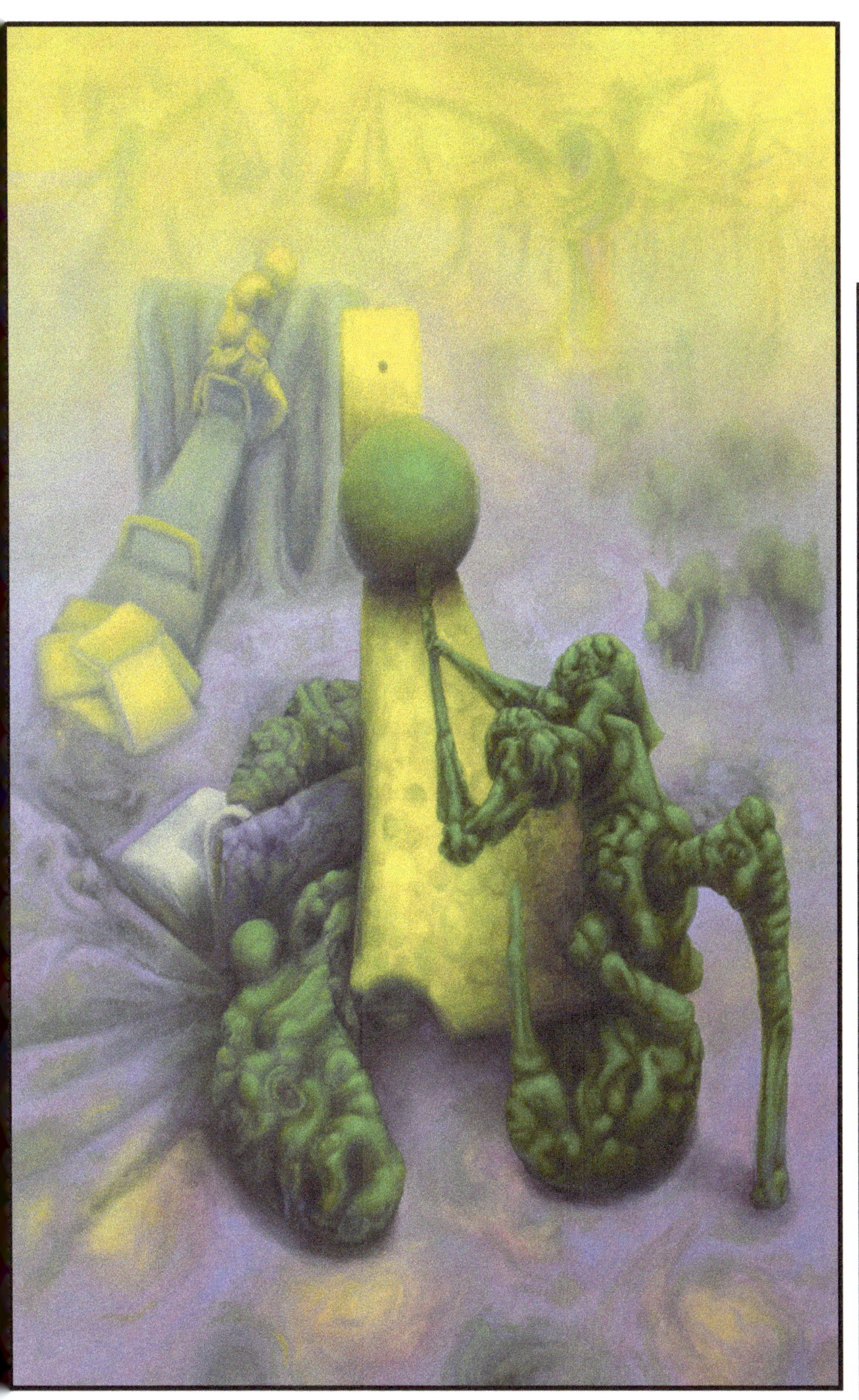

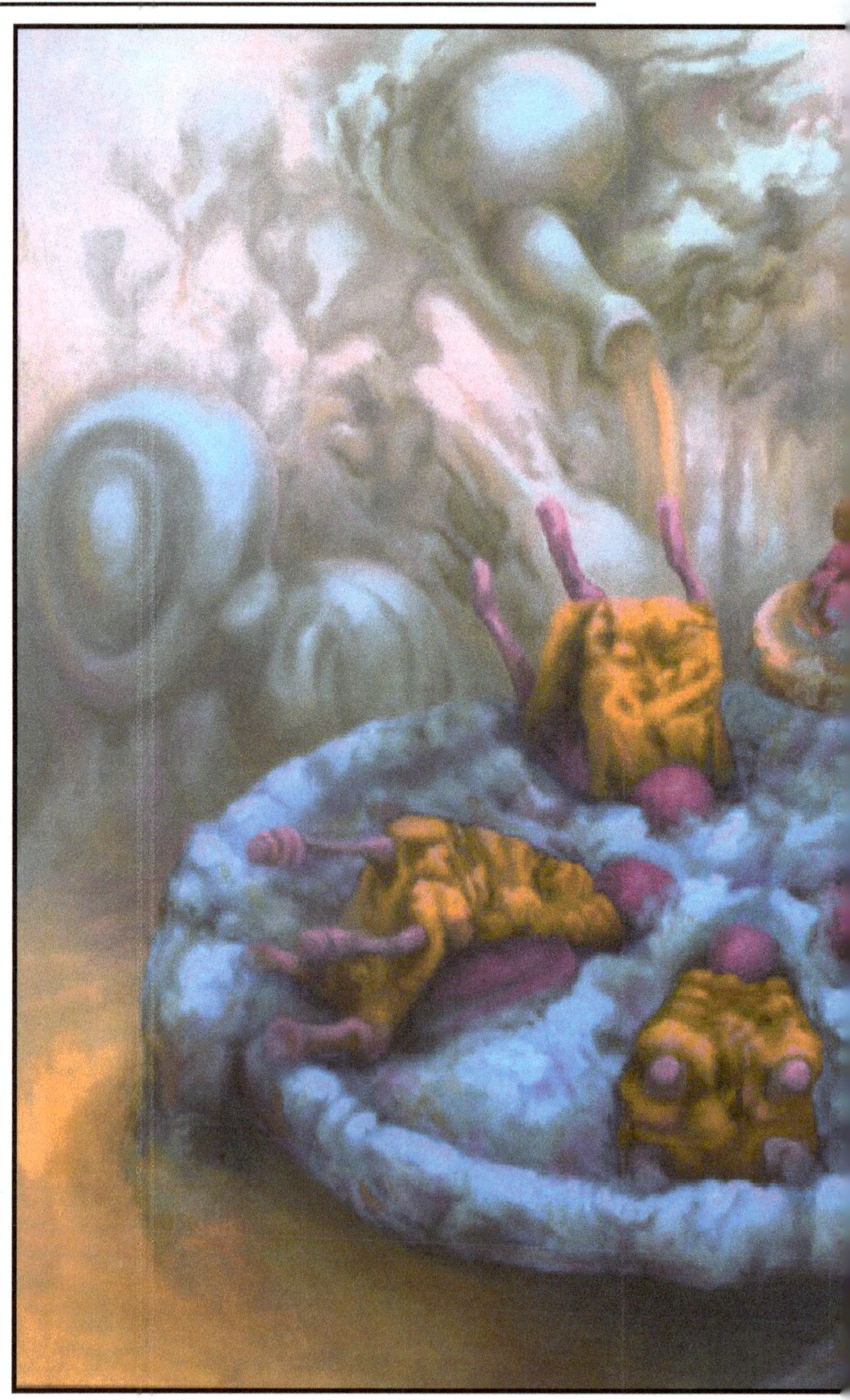

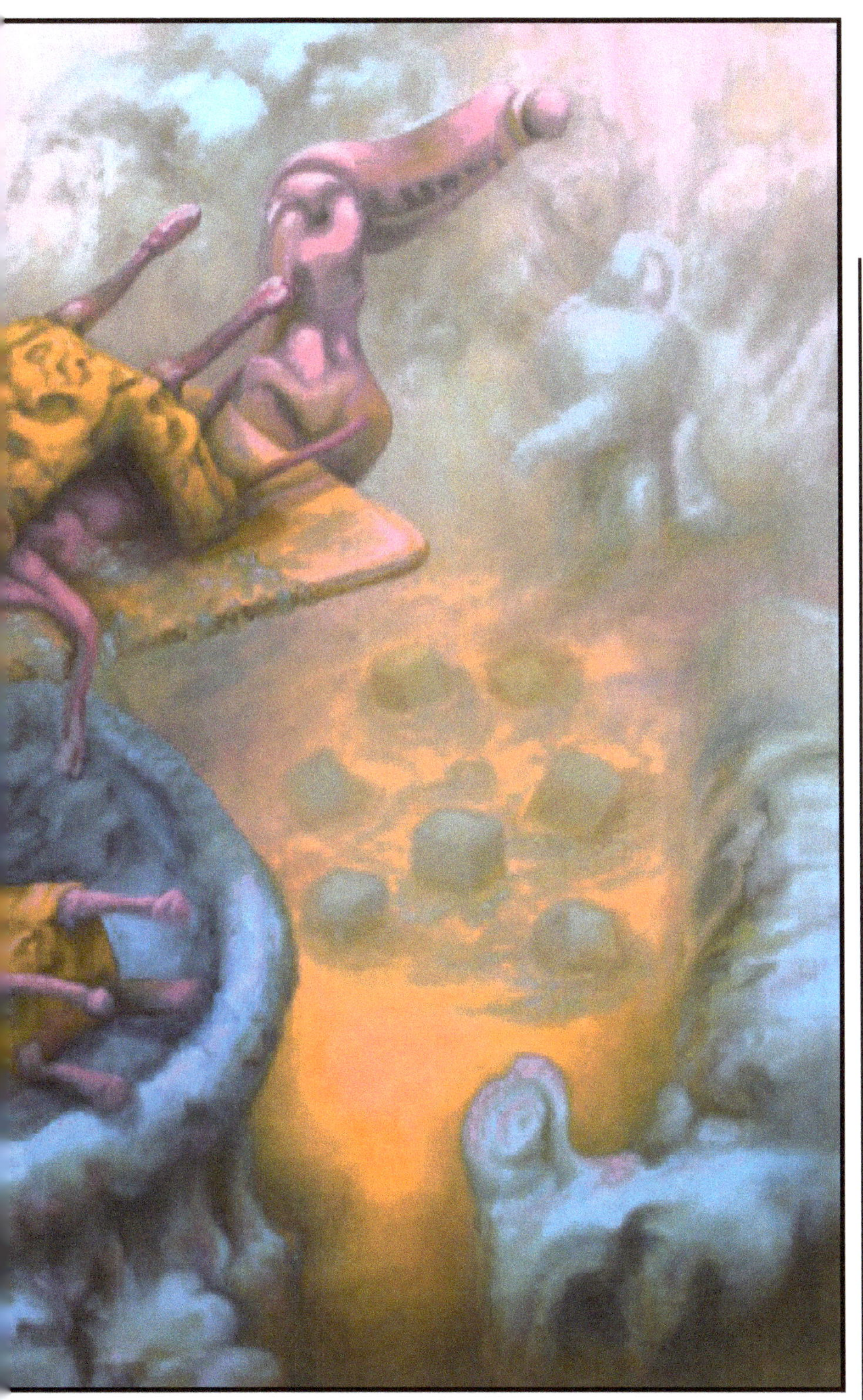

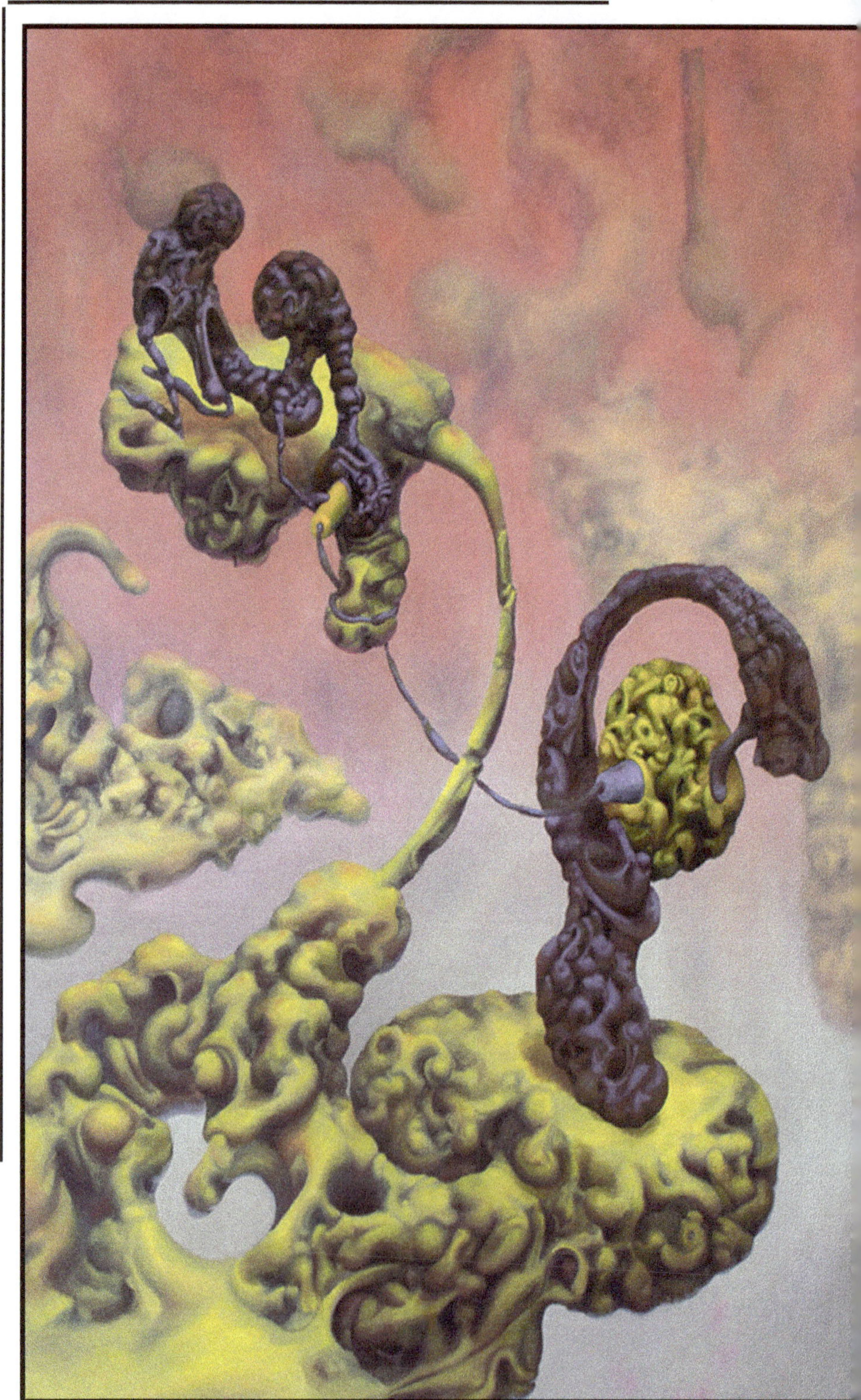

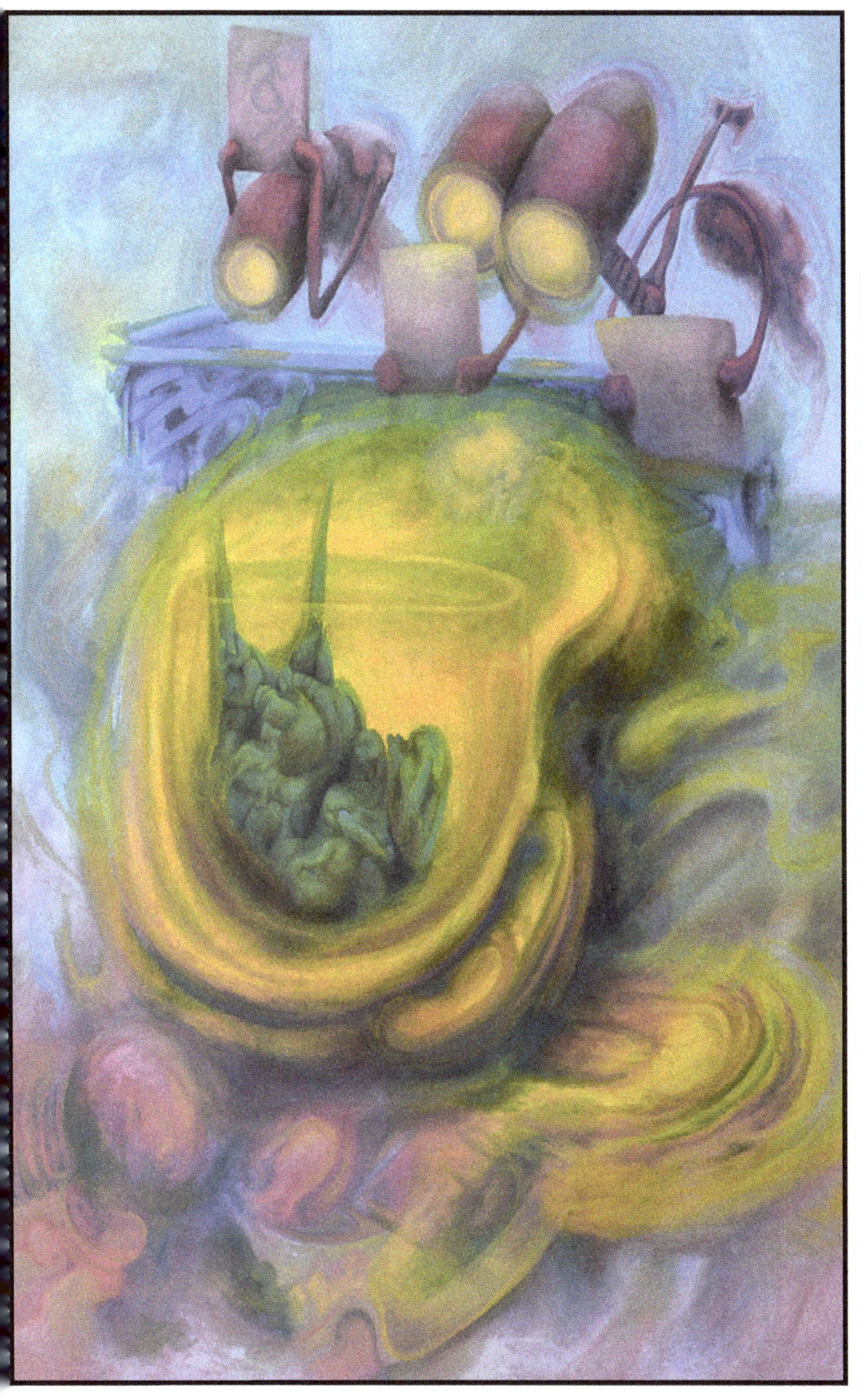

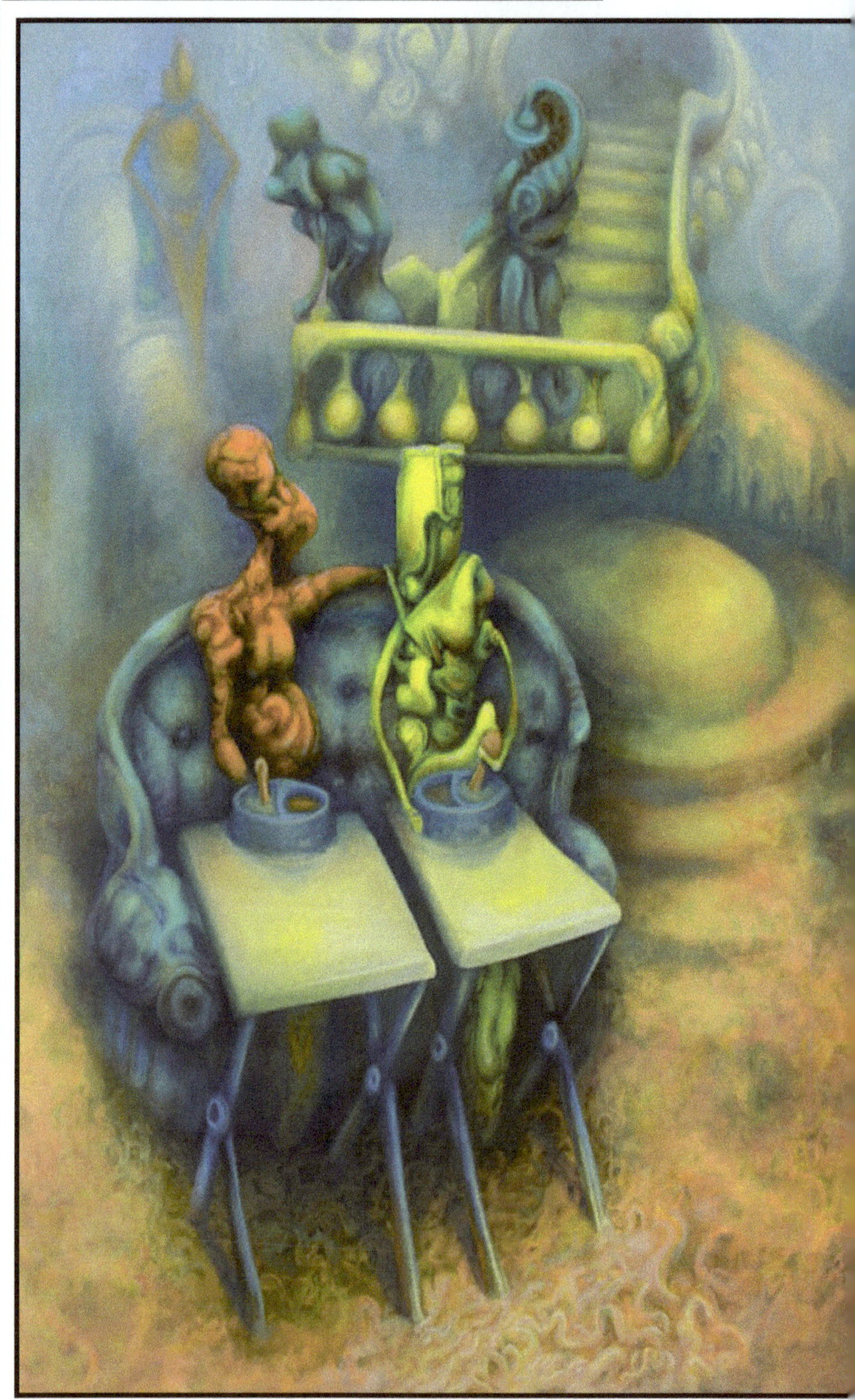

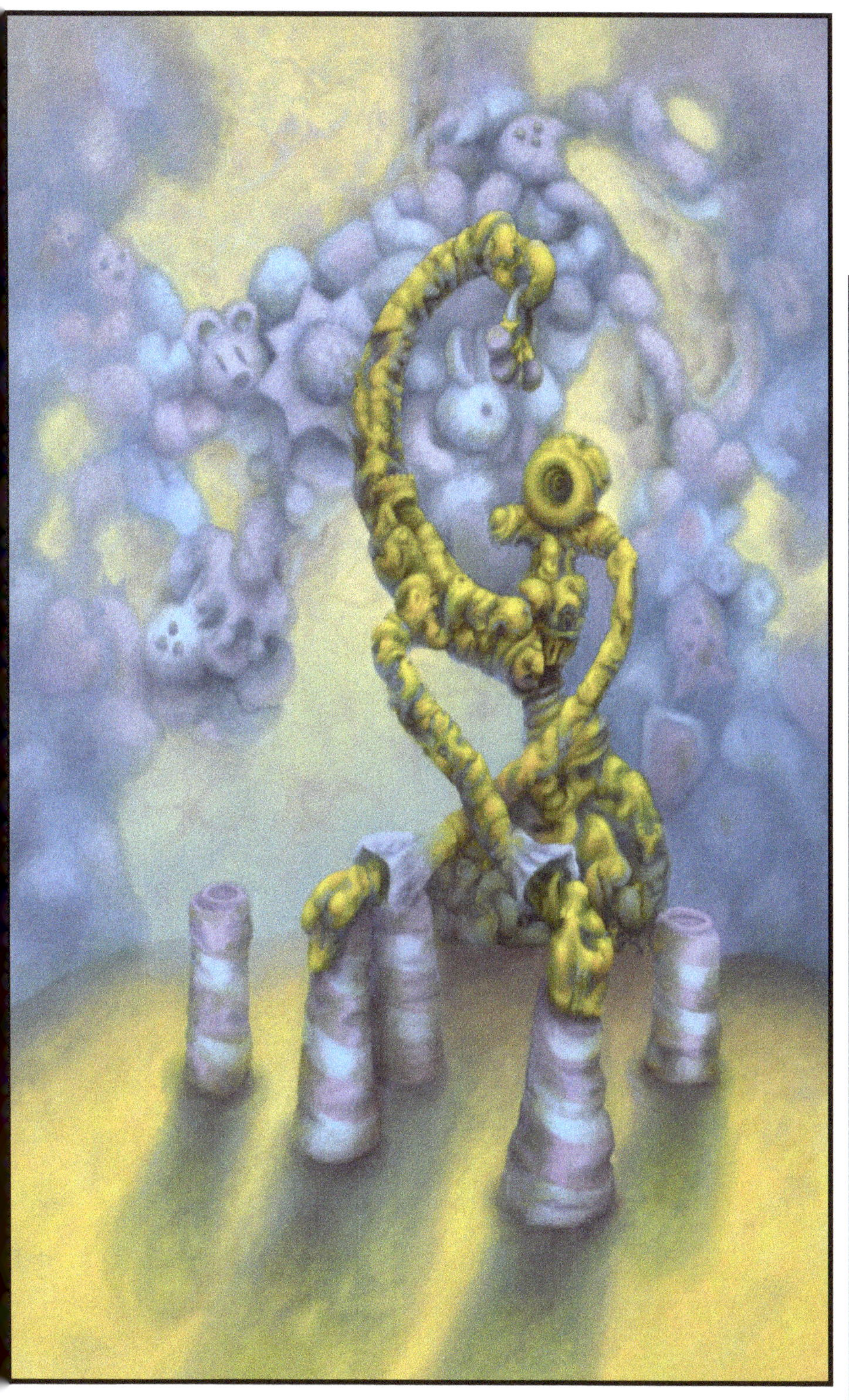

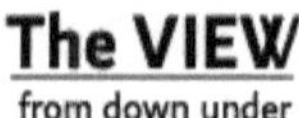

Garry Egger

HOSPITORATORY

Still reeling from his beanstalk/cow-trading fiasco, Jack took heart from 19[th]C goldfield workers who earned more from servicing miners, than the miners earned themselves. He thus developed the novel art of *hospitoratory* – 'hospitality with oratory'. His café, named '**JACK AND THE (HAS)BEENSTALK**,' had a la carte service and a stage where legends in their own minds, paid to share with the dining audience how '*the older they got the better they were!*' Jack was onto a winner. His fortune grew with the multitude of paying 'boomers' lined up to relate their (usually boring) memoirs to (usually overweight) diners who, in turn, paid (usually excessively) to over-eat. With his accumulating fortune, Jack grew beans sustainably, using the giant and the decaying stalk as fertiliser, thus satisfying his existential hiatus. After his youthful impetuosity, his mother's disappointment at his commercial savvy, and loss of the family cow, wasn't this a nice outcome?

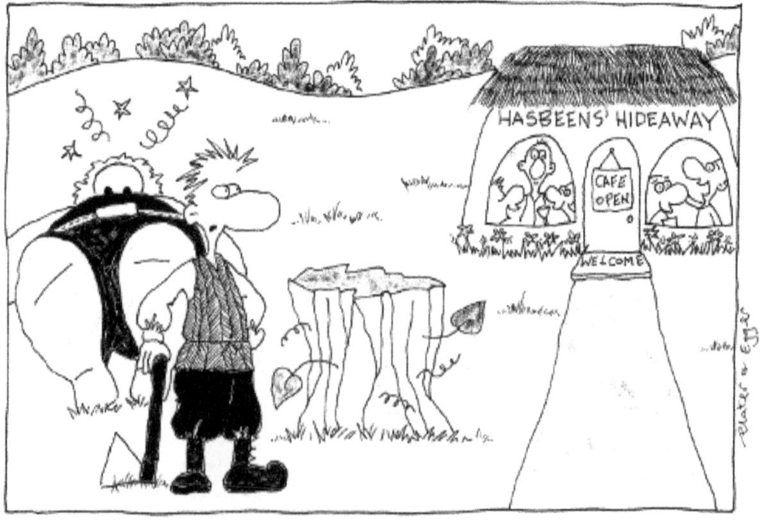

I used to think there was money in beans. But there's much more in 'has beens.'

AUTHOR'S PRIDE

He typed the last full stop and sat back. Content. Since retiring, he had applied himself to writing his memoirs ("*Between the (bottom) Lines*") because he knew, like all men of his ilk, that the world was waiting to hear of his exceptional life as an accountant. So, he gambled his pension on self-publishing – 50,000 copies for starters, but then to be more after these sold out. He had just enough left for a stall at the Vanity Publisher's Fair where, to his surprise, he was surrounded by similar retired aspirants striving for a second strike at life. ('*Shhhh...The Librarian's Tale*,' '*The Laying of Hands – on Bricks*,' '*Garbage in: Garbage Taken Out*'), He decided that he too was probably just ordinary. So, he bequeathed his publishing run to the Smith Family. At least they could recycle the paper. His life had not been totally wasted.

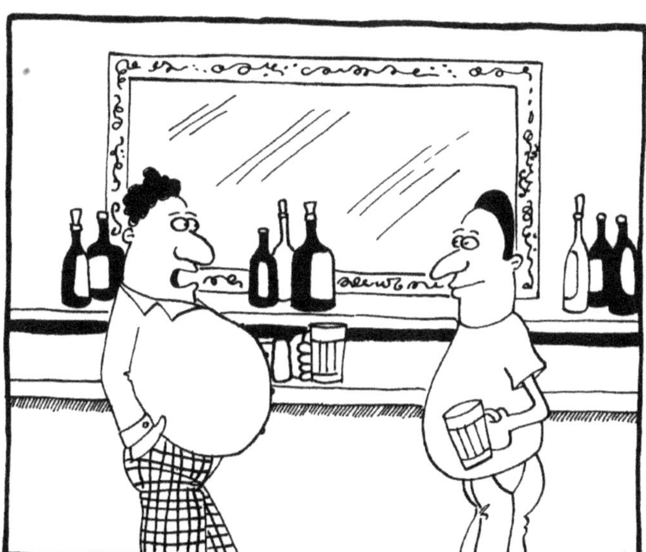

LIFE

The sponsors, 'Eternity Inc.', decided to settle it once and for all; the best definition of 'Life' – in <15 words. The judges; Frederich Nietzsche; Emanual Kant and Barach Spinoza had whittled down some commendable entries including Spike Milligan's: "... *occupational therapy between birth and death*," and Stephen Hawking's "(it)...*would be tragic if it weren't funny*" to three: John Lennon "(it's)...*what happens while you're busy making other plans*"; Einstein "(it's)... *like riding a bicycle. To keep your balance, you have to keep moving*" and Oscar Wilde: "*Life is too important to be taken seriously*". But as the judges went to announce the winner, Fred Nerk, a plasterer's mate from Bongongalong emerged holding a sign that read: "*Time Bends. Life Ends - Go Figure!*"The crowd went wild. Even Berty Einstein was happy. At least it incorporated his theory of matter which, like almost everybody, he never really understood anyway.

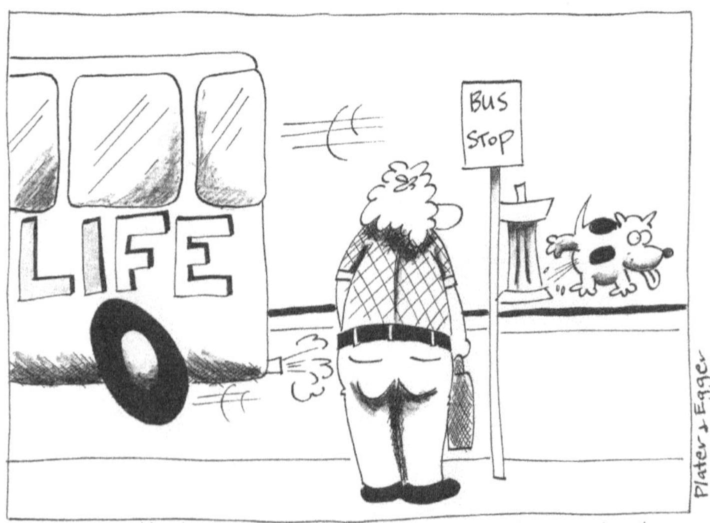

While his attention was diverted it just seemed to pass him by.

To: Enchanted Spirit 1111 Channeled Intuitive Clairaudient Tarot Reader on YouTube
Fr: A recently awakened from the dark night of the soul superfan

Amy Randall

Blessed Vista,

Gurl. I am manifesting so hard right now.

Clearly, my ancestors and Archangel Michael want abundance for me. And lots of it. I've watched like fifteen other readers today, and they all said vaguely the same thing you did, only with completely different cards, words, and meanings.

BTW, I love what you've done with your hair since the "What Spirit Wants You To Know" reading last week. Whoever posted that bangs were a bad idea must have low vibrational energies squared with Saturn. Their tower moment is coming, and you know I told her so in the comments. I got your back, sister.

Your fairy light, wolf spirit altar surrounded by that Boho chic tapestry fabric from Joanne's and the inspirational wood burned plaques feel like home. And I love how you change the flowers to suit the seasons. You'd never know they were plastic.

Quick question. If the mid-month financial reading is only for Cancer, sun, moon rising, ascendent, and cross watchers, isn't that pretty much everyone? I know it's a general reading. Maybe I didn't realize just how general.

Fingers crossed, someday I'll be able to afford a private reading with you. For now, I'll click on the link in the description box. Will I get on that email list where I receive, pretty much hourly, THINGS I NEED TO KNOW NOW, Tongue scraping detox tips, healing erectile dysfunction with anthracite crystals, and full moon past life sound bath get-togethers on Zoom?

Yes! Our community rocks!

So the first card out today was the Three of Rods. According to you, it means success or the beginning stages of success or the hope of the beginning stages of success or an abject failure that will lead to success. Totally resonates.

But the Six of Wands in the upright was a little confusing. You said there would be recognition. I haven't left my house in a year. Do you mean virtual recognition? Because I am totally speaking truth to power (thanks Queen of Wands) on our Customer Success Google meet-ups.

Summoning the spider energy you told me about, I'm really seeing Jamie for the first time. He's obviously my King of Pentacles. Did you say that it was a soul mate, twin flames connection in the Monthly Love Reading? Because I distinctly remember meeting him at a vomitorium just outside Rome, or was it Troy? It's a bit blurry, but my solar plexus chakra is vibrating with this memory, so it's definitely true.

Now I've smashed the like button for each of your videos, subscribed, and hit the wiggly bell so I can be notified every time you upload a new one. Boy, you're busy!

I even ordered your "It's in the cards, Bitches" hoodie that I can't wait to wear when we go up to the lake this summer. It sure will be great to get outside again. The wi-fi is not so good at our camp, but there's a Family Dollar about 15 miles away that gets a really strong signal, so don't worry, I'm not going anywhere.

Love and light,
Amy Randall
Your #1 Fan

Two Fables about Recovery

Alex Shapiro

For Tyrod Taylor and Alex Smith

The chilly pinch of a needle twinkling sterile skinny spearing the chest flesh
unsupported by bone and disappearing under the doctor's thumb, dispensing
enough numb into his bloodstream to convince the cracked ribs being cleaved
they're whole.

MORAL: Breathing gasps like his head's hooded in a plastic bag, his lung like a
tailspun jet spewing air meant for circulation.

Two seasons removed from a sack *crack* compounding his leg under retreat
from a pocket breached on hike by a blitz and an untouched end, alerts ping
subscriber screens urging us to tune in live for the only attendees wearing
Smith jerseys, his wife grimacing his children cheering at his ginger return
to the huddle interspliced with the QB he's replacing wincing off field, head
visible above the trainer team veiling his body.
He rehabbed on a military base, doctors peeling layers of infected tissue off
his mending tibia, days of digging for bacteria until the fresh reset bone was
fleshless, clean. His arm an occupational requirement, they transplanted
muscle from quad to calf, hoping merely to salvage the leg.
Half the line that tried protecting him last appearance intact, pressure comes
with constancy. Stiff tip toeing and quick screen passes manipulate blown
blocks almost as often as he's struck or buried by defenders. The scariest col-
lapse is Aaron Donald mounting full body weight atop his shoulder pads.

MORAL: When the clocks run out on a 20 point loss, his family is flashed mid
red faced exaltation at his reconstructed stride off the field.
In studio his resilience is commended, though experienced analysts note a
lack of crispness in his presence.

The Muezzin in Our Minaret

Photography by Christopher Ghattas

Poetry by Mike Wilson

The six o'clock sun, west of Istanbul,
scarved in red clouds, sheds light on
everything, on the Bosporus Bridge
behind, on me nested in Galata Tower,
gazing from Asia to Europe, smelling
centuries of blood, commerce, and the
simple taste of bread, countless lives lived
that meant something in their moments,
that still mean something in moments
like this;
       and it's only when we are raised
above the bustle by a Galata Tower and a
sunset do we hear the unceasing call to
prayer, to let loose our grip, to see
there is no God but God, yet in each
mundane sensation is the infinitely
important incarnation of the only One,
and there is no contradiction.

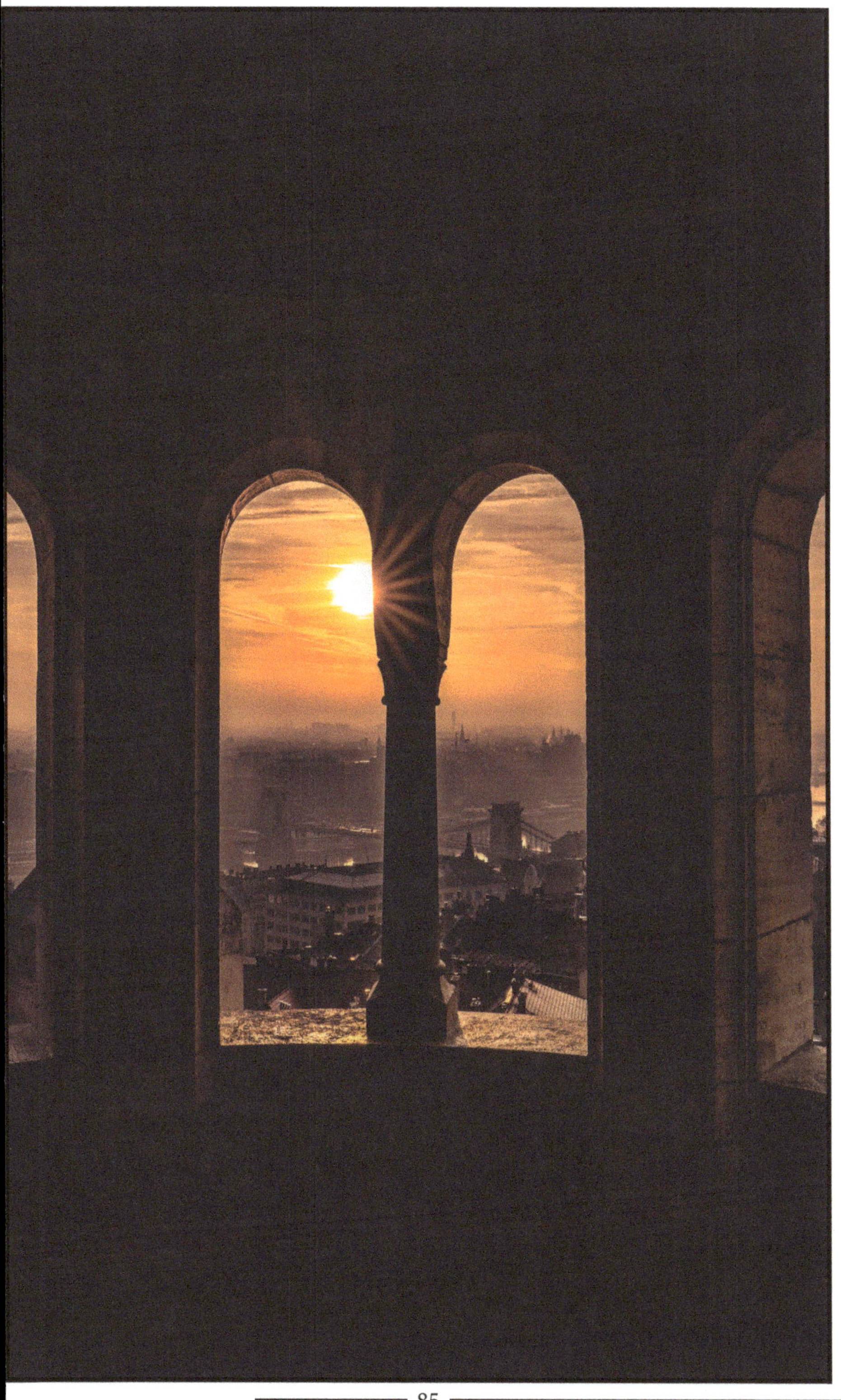

In Order Of Appearance:

Courtney Essary Messenbaugh is a writer and consultant who lives in Colorado and delights in the vast blue sky there. When she's not writing, you can find her tinkering at the piano, taking a bath, or spending time outside.

Steve grew up in England. Photography and natural science were the passions of his youth. After completing studies in physics at Liverpool University, Steve went on to work as an experimental physicist in Geneva, Switzerland. In 1987 he moved to the U.S. to teach physics at Harvard University. His scientific career eventually brought him to Chicago to work at Fermilab in Batavia, IL. It was in Chicagoland, at the time of the digital revolution, that Steve's photography really took off when he began selling stock images. In 2015 Steve joined the Perspective Gallery of Fine Art Photography in Evanston, Illinois. Steve is currently on the gallery's Board of Directors.
Steve plans his photographic projects carefully but they often start by happenstance when he sees some everyday thing in a new way. His photography is centered on creating what he likes to call imagination space.
Steve's favorite photographer quotes are from Elliott Erwitt who once said of photography: "I've found it has little to do with the things you see and everything to do with the way you see them" and from Robert Doisneau who said of the photographic process that "We must always remember that a picture is also made up of the person who looks at it … You offer the seed and then the viewer grows it inside himself."
In recent years Steve has had his work featured in photography magazines, published in books and exhibited in galleries in the United States and Europe. His featured exhibitions at the Perspective Gallery have been: Chicago through the Looking Glass (February 2016), From the Ground Up (April 2017), One-sixth of a Second (February 2018), Discarded (June 2019), and River Ice (February 2020). Steve currently lives in downtown Chicago.
Website: www.stevegeer.com
Instagram: stevegeer.photography

Vanessa Grixti is an emerging poet originally from Toronto, Canada. She has lived abroad for two years, previously in Costa Rica and currently in Mexico.
@vanessagrixti

Natalia A. Pagán Serrano is a poet from Puerto Rico. She currently resides in Oregon, drenched in tree-magic and rain, with her fiancé, Daniel, and her cat, Esteban. When not writing, you can find Natalia making soup.
Instagram handle: @n.a.pagan

Kathryn Matheson's first book of poetry, Cold Strawberries, was published in 2014. She remembers writing her first poem at age 13 and has spent every spare moment since then reading, writing and breathing poetry. Matheson, now 25, lives and works in New York City. She is currently in the process of writing her second book and has a poem forthcoming in HASH Journal.

Will Dolben is an American screenwriter, producer and poet.
He holds a master's in screenwriting from the University of Southern California.
He was a quarterfinalist in the prestigious Academy of Motion Picture Arts and Sciences international screenwriting competition.

Jeremiah Gilbert is an award-winning photographer, writer, and avid traveler based out of Southern California. He likes to travel light and shoot handheld. His travels have taken him to nearly a hundred countries and territories around the globe. His photography has been published internationally, in both digital and print publications, and has been exhibited worldwide, including in Leica's LFI Gallery. His hope is to inspire those who see his work to look more carefully at the world around them in order to discover beauty in unusual and unexpected places. He is also the author of the collection Can't Get Here from There: Fifty Tales of Travel. He can be found on Instagram @jg_travels

Robert McDonald's work has appeared previously in Columbia Poetry Review, Sentence, Court Green, PANK, and Bending Genres, among many other journals and zines. Robert lives in Chicago, and works at an independent bookstore. Follow Robert on Instagram @robmcwriter

Chris Andrews, who teaches at Western Sydney University, has published two collections of poems – Cut Lunch (Indigo, 2002) and Lime Green Chair (Waywiser, 2012, winner of the Anthony Hecht Poetry Prize) – and translated books of prose fiction, including César Aira's How I Became a Nun (New Directions, 2007) and Selva Almada's The Wind that Lays Waste (Graywolf, 2019).

Paul Reynolds is a Virginia based visual artist, writer, and musician, whose visual work usually grapples with experimental figurative studies and portraiture, exploring the human form and visage as a matter of encounter. He is interested in representation, gesture, mark making, and language, as all these phenomena converge to depict and divulge our subjective and objective worlds, augmenting our self-understanding.

Melinda Freudenberger received her MFA in Poetry from The New School. Her poems have recently appeared in the New Delta Review and Always Crashing magazine, and are forthcoming in Anomaly. She is an Associate Poetry Editor at West Trade Review. You can find more of her work on her website: melindafreudenberger.com. Instagram handle: @poetpopstar

Kirsten Hemmy's first book of poetry was a Tom Lombardo selection from Press 53. Her work has recently appeared in Glass, Your Impossible Voice, Killing the Buddha, Pine Row Press, CaKe, Panoply and elsewhere. A Tedx performer and Fulbright fellow, Hemmy currently lives in the Sultanate of Oman where she teaches creative writing.

Diamante Lavendar lives in the Midwest US. Her art is created in regard to the themes of spirituality and the human condition. She enjoys using art as a medium to explore the issues of life and the human reactions to those issues with a strong emphasis on spirituality. Many of her works are also abstract in nature with a focus on color, shapes, and lines. The majority of her work is mixed media digital art which includes some or all of the following: photography, fractals, drawing, painting, and digital art.
Diamante's work has been shown in numerous online and "brick and mortar" exhibitions and has been awarded in many of those shows. She has also been recognized in the American Art Awards in 2017, 2018, 2019 and 2020. Diamante's work has been published in several magazines including Edge Of Faith Magazine, Eris and Eros, The Closed Eye Open and Beyond Words Literary Magazine. Her work can be viewed on her website at www.diamante-lavendar.pixels.com.
Instagram-@diamantelavendar

CANDICE KELSEY teaches writing in Los Angeles. Her poetry appears in Poets Reading the News and Poet Lore among other journals. Her first collection, Still I am Pushing, was released last March. She won the 2019 Two Sisters Writing's Contest, received Honorable Mention for Common Ground's 2019 Poetry Contest, and was nominated for both a Best of the Net and a Pushcart. Find her at www.candicemkelseypoet.com and @candicekelsey1.

Alex Mepham (they/them) is a PhD student investigating how background noise impacts speech understanding. Alex writes and translates poetry and short prose, with work appearing in Magma, Beyond Words Literary Magazine, and Modern Poetry in Translation. Alex currently lives in York, UK, and can be found at amepham.carrd.co.

Chris Boyko is an Atlanta-based automatist surrealist artist whose paintings are characterized by a highly imaginative interpretation of the everyday world. He received a Bachelor of Fine Arts degree from Kennesaw State University in 2014.
@boykoart

Garry Egger MPH PhD is an Australian academic and writer with over 30 books and 250 scientific articles to his credit. He has teamed with cartoonist Suzanne Plater to provide 150 word (exactly) satirical pieces on political, social and behavioral issues under the heading of 'the View' (from down under) Attached are three of these previously unpublished pieces.

Amy asks that you please not follow her on social media during these turbulent times.

Alex Wells Shapiro is a poet and artist from the Hudson Valley, living in Chicago. He reads submissions for Another Chicago Magazine and Frontier Poetry, and is a co-founder of Exhibit B: A Reading Series presented by The Guild Literary Complex. His work is recently published or forthcoming in Blood Tree Literature, streetcake, Pangyrus, and The Indianapolis Review. More of his work may be found at www.alexwellsshapiro.com.

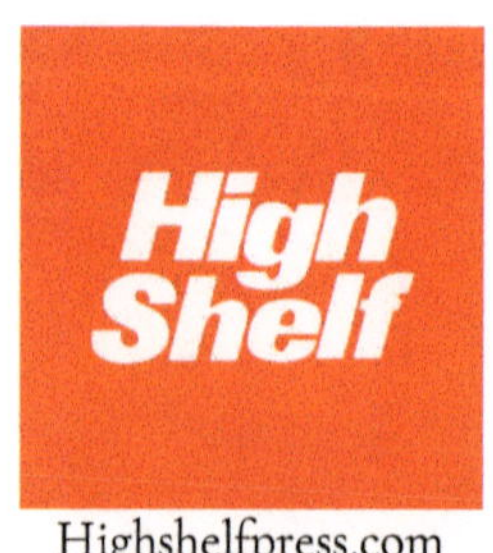

Highshelfpress.com